ACCOUNTS

OF

RELIGIOUS REVIVALS

IN MANY PARTS OF THE

UNITED STATES

FROM 1815 TO 1818.

Collected from numerous Publications, and
Letters from Persons of piety and
correct information.

BY JOSHUA BRADLEY, A. M.
ALBANY, N. Y.

The Lord hath done great things for us.
He hath not dealt so with any nation.
Declare his doings among the people.
                                    SCRIPTURE.

Richard Owen Roberts, Publishers
Wheaton, Illinois
1980

PUBLISHED IN 1819
BY G. J. LOOMIS & CO.
OF ALBANY, NEW YORK

REPRINTED IN 1980
BY RICHARD OWEN ROBERTS, PUBLISHERS
WHEATON, ILLINOIS 60187

Printed in the United States of America

PREFACE.

Pure religion is of infinite importance to man. It not only discloses the odiousness of sin, but the benevolence of God in sending his Son into the world to save all them that believe. Wherever it is received, souls are reconciled unto God, through the atoning merits of Jesus, and abound in joys unutterable.

Prophets and Apostles have specified the times and places in which the Spirit moved upon the hearts of many, and brought them from darkness into marvellous light. Since their days, the servants of Jesus in every age have testified of the descent of the Spirit and its influences upon mankind. Since 1790, almost every State in America has been blessed with revivals.

To embody all that has appeared in various forms since this glorious work commenced would fill many volumes. The writer, therefore, presumes that this small book compiled from numerous accounts of revivals since the commencement of 1815 to 1818, with the addition of some that have not been published, may be acceptable to thousands. This work will be put into the hands of multitudes, who have not read the magazines that abound in our country. And many who read them, may wish to obtain this work. that is solely designed to bring to view from a cloud of witnesses, the agency of the Spirit in regeneration. As this is his design, he flatters himself, that no individual, that no denomination of Christians, will be offended at his leaving out of the accounts presented him for publication, every thing that he considers inconsistent with the best intentions of his heart, to make this volume bear a rich variety of declarations of peace, harmony and good will to men.

With gratitude he acknowledges the reception of many excellent letters upon revivals from ministers of different denominations, and more than two thousand subscribers. May it please Him who died for sinners, still to appear in his glory to build up Zion, until the whole earth is filled with the knowledge of his salvation, and all nations bow before him, and call him blessed.

With sentiments of high esteem, I beg leave to subscribe myself the publick's affectionate friend, and the church's devoted servant.

JOSHUA BRADLEY.

Albany, (*N. Y.*) *Feb.* 1819.

The names of ministers who have either sent me letters upon revivals, or from whose compositions, that have appeared before the publick, I have made extracts, are Rev. Dr. Green, President of N. J. College.

Dr. J. Coe	B. Titcomb
Dr. Clarke	J. Tripp
P. Cook	S. Sterns
D. Dodge	P. Crosby
H. Marshall	N. Dodge
S. Goodale	J. Higbee
O. Robinson	R. Cushman
S. Dexter	J. Elliot
E. Hunting	H. Dickson
T. Rand	B. Lane
D. Merrill	E. Hebard
B. Perkins	M. Thomas
J. Spalding	C. Phileo
L. Parsons	W. Wisner
C. Fuller	J. Jefferies
A. Jackson	C. Ten Eych
J. Bostwick	J. D. Gardiner
A. Messer	S. Luckey
A. Parmelee	A. Bennet
F. Fisk	L. Hall
H. Chapman	S. G. Roszel
J. Peck	W. Richards
O. Osgood	N. Dutton.

I have not only made use of the writings of these ministers of different denomina-

‌

tions; but also of the narratives of Synods, Presbyteries, Conventions, Associations, and every publication, upon revivals that has come within my knowledge, and the plan of my book.

———

Names of towns in which revivals have spread their benign influences.

RELIGIOUS REVIVALS,

From 1815, to 1818.

ACWORTH, (N. H.)

NOTHING has appeared like a revival in this town until 1814. In this year the Rev. P. Cook was ordained. At the first communion after his consecration, sixteen offered themselves to the church. Immediately after this, instances of individual conviction made their appearance in different parts of the society and one and another were made to rejoice in God. A solemn and strict attention was paid to the word preached, and the good work progressed gradually until Sept. 1816. In which time about sixty were added to the church. Every seat in the house of God was filled, not with drowsy inattentive hearers, but with awakened immortals, hanging on the lips of the speaker with almost breathless attention; looking as if

B

their everlasting all depended on the proper improvement of a single sermon. Neither were the people satisfied with attending merely on the duties of the sanctuary. Conference meetings were established in different parts of the society, and were attended with increasing interest. About this time our winter schools began: and several of them enjoyed the singular blessing of pious young men to instruct them. Feeling that responsibility, which every guardian of youth who knows the worth of the soul will feel, they blended divine with human learning; and while they were careful in teaching the "young idea how to shoot," they were no less anxious that its first growth should be heavenward.

In a school in the western part of the society. a regular course of biblical instruction was introduced. Questions were proposed weekly, and one evening in each week set apart for their discussion. The answers to these questions were required in scriptural language. As soon as this mode of instruction was introduced, a visible alteration was seen in many scholars. They began to discover a greater relish for the scriptures. In searching for the answers to their questions, they felt an increasing desire to know more of the lively oracles of divine truth. Every vacant moment when relieved from their other school exercises, the bible was taken up, and the unheeded tear which now and then would drop over the sacred page, showed that its precious sentiments penetrated their hearts. On Tuesday evening, Jan. 14, 1817, when assembled as usual for the discussion of their scriptural questions, occurred a scene on which memory dwells with delight; and which no doubt excited those fresh acclamations of joy in heaven, which takes place on the return of every penitent sinner.

The house on a sudden became a little Pentecost. The first question which was asked a young woman of twenty years of age, was, What is regeneration? She

rose, attempted to answer, failed, and sunk
under the weight of a wounded spirit. The
next in order was called upon, but was
unable to reply, from the same cause as
the former. The third issued in the same
manner; and in a few minutes the whole
school consisting of about twenty six, were
overwhelmed in a flood of penitent grief:
and cries such as these were heard in every
part of the room; How can I live! what
shall I do! God be merciful to me a sinner! With these were mingled the pressing anxious request, Do dear master,
pray for me—pray for me in particular.

In this scene of general distress, the
master, though no stranger at the throne
of grace, and who had previously attended
prayers in his school daily, was too much
agitated by the occasion to govern his passions to commend his pupils to the Lord
Jesus. At this time there was sitting in
the midst of this weeping assembly, a young
man, who was remarkably delivered from
the dominion of sin, and made a trophy of

redeeming love a few days before: who
had but just found a throne of grace for
humble suppliants to approach: and who
possessed no distinguishing qualifications
to fit him to recommend his despairing
school-mates to the mercy of God.—Seeing
the purturbation of the master, and the
distress which prevailed on every side, he
rose, and with apparent composure said,
Let us pray. He prayed: and it was
evident God heard: for he was an instrument of his own choosing. A modest youth,
naturally diffident, a new born soul of yes-
terday, committing in language perfectly
appropriate, the wants of his distressed
companions to that wonder-working God,
who alone is able to forgive sins, and im-
part spiritual life to the soul. It was a
scene sufficiently interesting to rouse from
lethargy the most stupid sinner and kindle within him a lively sensation of the
day of judgment. When this prayer was
ended, the master had so far recovered
himself, as to be able to offer up a fervent

petition in behalf of his school.   When he closed, it was thought expedient to invite some of the neighbours to come and behold, this exhibition of the terrours of the Lord. Two men. professors, who had children in the school, were called.   One of these next took his turn in prayer. After some conversation, the forementioned young man, next the master. then the neighbour, each a second time sought in prayer for that grace which alone could help in such a time of need. By this time the evening was far spent, and proposals were made to retire.   But the scholars unanimously, were unwilling to leave the house or separate from each other. The impression which seized their minds, seemed to be, that it would be departing from the immediate presence of Jehovah.— The exclamation of Jacob was strikingly verrified ; And he was afraid and said, how dreadful is this place! this is none other but the house of God, and this is the gate of heaven.   After much intreaty, they were, however, persuaded to go home to their respective families.

Next morning, information being received of what had taken place. a conference meeting was appointed at 1 o'clock, P. M. Here was a spectacle presented which must have excited the admiration of angels. Each scholar holding in his hand the Bible, Testament, or Watts' psalms and hymns, and searching for his life for that spiritual bread which if a man eat, he shall live for ever. The assembly was large. During this meeting, many became convinced of their lost condition, and began to think it high time to awake out of sleep, and call on God before they perished. On this melting occasion, the stoutest heart seemed to dissolve like wax before an increasing fire. The Friday evening following, the weekly conference returned in the centre district. Here at an early hour was presented the little band, literally clad in the armour of the gospel : holding in their hands the sure directory to eternal life. It was proposed that each scholar should read some passage, psalm or hymn, descriptive of the state of his mind. Some by this time were delivered from the burden of sin, which had so heavily pressed them down, and that hope which brings comfort to every true believer in Jesus, had begun to irradiate the soul.—This was known from the subject read. To hearts like these, the sentiments contained in the 136th Ps. C. M. were found to be in perfect unison, as were those of the 51st Ps. to many others, who seemed overwhelmed by the waves of contrition; whose tremulous voices faltered as they read. and often before the subject was ended, died away in the silence of grief. It must be confessed, that the christian spectator needed a moments reflection, to determine whether the ground on which he stood was purely earthly. It was evident that the Holy Spirit was there. Many while the scholars were reading received for the first time in their hearts, a pointed arrow from the quiver of the Almighty, and like their fellow sufferers on the day of Pentecost were led to cry out, Men and brethren, what shall we do? The work spread powerfully.

Next morning another school in the east part of the town assembled for their usual school exercises; and it was soon discovered that the master was completely incapacitated to proceed with his ordinary instructions, on account of the weight of conviction which lay on his mind. Fifteen of his eldest scholars were immediately in a similar situation, and in a short time the neighbours were called to attend this solemn vision. and the school was transformed into a religious conference; and continued thus until night. For sometime after this. not a day returned, without the joyful tidings that some one was convicted, or some one made happy by being reconciled to God through the merits of a Saviour.

This revival spread its benign influences into other schools, and many souls in this town have given evidences that they were sealed for heaven. May parents feel the importance of choosing pious instructors for their children, and may the ministers of Christ be clothed with salvation.

———

WILMINGTON, (Del.) 1815.

This work made its appearance, agreeably to God's usual way, of gathering souls under the banners of his abounding grace. The Rev. Mr. Dodge was a distinguished instrument of awakening sinners. His brethren were brought into great distress and perplexity, and expected that their pastor would leave them to manage their differences without his personal attendance. Amid their tribulation, they were enabled to call on God. He heard their prayers; frustrated the calculated removal of Mr. D. poured out his spirit among them: settled the church again in her o y, and crowded their house of worship with souls, who trembled at the word and cried for mercy. Mr. D. was soon so deeply impressed with this singular display of divine power, that he was constrained to alter his former arrangements about leaving the place, and enter with all his strength into the work that increased around him.

Every event seemed to augment the concern of multitudes. The sudden death of a young man alarmed many. They viewed themselves advancing with all possible rapidity towards the dreary mansions of unalterable misery. Their impressions were so great, that many were scarcely able to leave the house where weeping, and sighs and prayers abounded. Meetings were frequent. Preaching, singing, praying, and exhorting became very pleasant work. The children of God were refreshed, and engaged in the revival with increasing ardour.

Ministers who visited this place, caught the fires of the sanctuary, and preached Jesus with power. The sitting of the Delaware Association afforded the people much entertainment. This was a solemn sea-

son. Many were wounded in their hearts.
—Such a vast concourse attended, that the
doors, windows. aisles, stair-cases, and
yard, were full; and a large number went
away, who could not get near enough to
hear the speakers: the work went on so
powerfully, that it became impracticable to
dismiss the people as usual. Many would
meet Mr. D at the pulpit stairs, crying for
mercy, often obliging him to spend one or
two hours after preaching in conversation.
One day while he was speaking, one of his
deacons informed him, there were some
young men in the gallery who were so
much affected, they could not leave the
house, and wished him to go up and converse with them. He crowded along the
aisle, speaking to many, till he came to the
foot of the stairs, which he ascended; and,
O! who can tell the feelings of his heart in
seeing a number of young men pouring out
the penitential tear, and each one saying,
*I fear I have sinned so much, I can never
be forgiven!* The people crowded up from

below, and about an hour was spent in preaching Christ unto them. This was none other than the house of God and the gate of heaven.

The happy subjects of this work have been principally youths from 14 to 25 years of age. One of only 11 years obtained a comfortable hope. The experience of this child was very interesting. One day after relating many things, much to the satisfaction of Mr. D. he interrogated her thus; How does your past life appear in your view? She replied, O very black. Do you feel a hatred to your former ways? Yes, Sir, I do feel a great hatred to them. Why do you hate them? Because God hates them. Do you think God would be just to send you to hell for your sins? Yes, Sir, I do, and wonder he has not done it long ago. How do you expect to be saved? Through the Lord Jesus Christ. How does Christ appear in your view? O! very precious; one altogether lovely. Do you feel so much love for Jesus that you could for-

C

sake all for him? O yes, Sir, I could forsake father, and mother, and all my brothers, and sisters, for him, and every thing
else in the world. This work spread among
other congregations. The Rev. Messrs.
Blackburn and Patterson, of the Presbyterian denomination were greatly blessed in
their visit and preaching in this place. The
Spirit descended, and every cheek appeared bathed in tears, and many cried, What
shall we do to be saved. The people
might truly say, on that occasion:

Let all with thankful hearts confess,
Thy welcome messengers of peace;
Thy power in their report be found,
And let thy feet behind them sound.

NORTH HAVEN, (Conn.)
The Baptist Society in this town was organized by the author. The spirit descended upon it and about fifty were hopefully converted in 1810 and 1811. In June

1811, a respectable council of ministers and delegates convened and gave the young converts approbation as a church. The revival continued gradually for nearly two years. In 1813 the author moved to Vermont, and they remained destitute of a pastor until 1817. Yet they held meetings regularly every Lord's day, and enjoyed the gifts of ministers more than half of the time.

Darkness began to cover the people, and every professor complained of stupidity. They felt unwilling to live at this cold distance, from the life cheering beams of the sun of righteousness. Therefore, some more sensibly affected, than others, with a sense of their backslidings, and God's usual way of visiting his people, proposed to spend a day in fasting and prayer. A day was appointed, and the church and a few others assembled. This was in Sept. 1815. He who never was absent when his people unite to pray, made them feel the weight of their sins. They sighed and wept, not only

for their own souls, but for the conversion
of others.   Two young women were awakened at this meeting.   The church began
to revive.   From this time two conference
meetings were attended in a week. These
meetings were soon crowded, and many
souls were moved to cry for mercy.   The
exhortations of the brethren were greatly
blessed. Ministers were called to visit this
people; and, blessed be God, they came
in the name of Him, who is exalted as a
Prince and a Saviour, for to give repentance to Israel, and forgiveness of sins.
They could say. Our gospel came not unto
you in word only, but also, in power, and
in the Holy Ghost, and in much assurance.
   The Rev Messrs. Blakesly. Bently,
Talmage, Miller. Bolles of Tolland, and
many others, came over and laboured to
the satisfaction of saints, and the alarming
of the ungodly.   These ministers were instrumental in building up zion in this
town.   Mr. Blakesly, being the first who
came, after the commencement of the re-

vival, was most distinguishingly owned and crowned with success. He spent much time in preaching, visiting, and exhorting, from house to house. The power of God was felt in every part of the society. Every meeting was numerous, although the roads, storms, and other circumstances attendant on the seasons, combined like an army to garrison the people in their houses.

In the time of this refreshing from the presence of the Lord many experienced renovating grace, and about 40 joined the church. This work like most awakenings, was principally among the youths; yet, there were two or three instances of conversion among those of 30 or 40 years old. This people still continue in spiritual prosperity. O Lord, save thy people, and bless thine inheritance; feed them also, and lift them up for ever.

SALISBURY, (N. H.)

A number of Christians in this place held a prayer meeting every week for some

time before the revival began.   In July
1815, they were much encouraged in be-
seeching the Lord to revive his work ; for
several young women who were employed
in school keeping, were so deeply impressed that they were obliged to dismiss their
pupils for some time, not being able to
discharge the duties expected from them.
The Holy Spirit was sent to apply the
balm of rich grace to their wounded hearts.

The work soon spread with great rapidity : ball-rooms and other scenes of
amusement were deserted. The still small
voice of truth made its way to the heart
without exciting noise or enthusiasm.

In the commencement of the revival a
girl of 12 years, being in great distress,
said at the close of one of the meetings ;
O how much precious time I have spent
in vanity ! How can the Lord have mercy
on so great a sinner ! In a short time the
Lord bestowed delivering grace, and her
tongue uttered praise to her exalted Redeemer.   Many united with her in walk-

ing in the paths of wisdom, and professing Jesus before men.

The ordinances of the gospel were attended with great solemnity, and peculiarly blessed to numbers. In less than two months 49 were added to the Baptist, and a considerable number to the Congregational church in this town. When the Lord shall build up zion, he shall appear in his glory.

SEDGWICH and BLUEHILL, (Me.)

Previously to the work's beginning in these towns, the Lord had shed some mercy drops upon those westward. The brethren appointed meetings of fasting and prayer, and the work appeared to progress towards the East.

In Feb. 1816, the Baptist minister in Nobleborough, came on a visit to Bluehill. Under his preaching the work soon became visible. Its progress was so rapid, that it soon extended into every part of the town. It was solemn and still; but remarkably powerful. Its subjects were children, youths, and the middle aged. Now, multitudes of thoughtless, giddy youths, who, just before, were engaged in the height of vanity, were seen flocking to meetings every day. They seemed to pay the utmost attention to the precious word of God, that was preached among them.

In April it began in Sedgwich and spread in every part of the town, and into many of the adjoining towns. The oldest Christians in that region say, they never saw a work of grace equal to this, since the Eastern shores were inhabited. They have seen reformations equally powerful, but none before so extensive, and so free from inconsistency and confusion. It was enough to affect the most hardened infidel, to attend the prayer meetings of the youths and children, and to behold the order they maintained. Their prayers and exhortations were short, but generally to the purpose, and very spiritual. These meetings have been remarkably instrumental in awakening those who were going on the way to ruin. In a few months 150 have been added to this church, and a considerable number to the congregational church. 104 to the Baptist church in Bluehill, and about 30 to the Congregational church in that place. The good work spread into a number of towns, of which I have not obtained sufficient information to give the publick correct accounts.

How charming is the place,
  Where my Redeemer God,
Unveils the beauties of his face,
  And sheds his love abroad!

Not the fair palaces,
  To which the great resort,
Are once to be compar'd with this,
  Where Jesus holds his court.

THOMASTON, (Me.) 1816.

When the Rev. Mr. Baker was first settled in this town, he found, that the young
people were very much given to lightness
and profanity. To change their morals
and render them amiable in society, he introduced a sunday school, which soon had
the desired effect. Early on that blessed
morning prayer meetings were appointed
and well attended. Also, one conference
meeting on a week day evening.

The precious Saviour, ever ready to bless
the endeavours of his people, soon gave
encouragement to these well laid plans,
and these noble exertions, by pouring out
his Holy Spirit upon his servants and hand-
maidens. Their meetings became large
and very solemn. There, the deep sigh of
the anxious, the silent tear of the humble
penitent, and the joyful thanksgiving of
such as were delivered from the bondage
of sin, formed a very interesting scene.
Christians were constrained to exclaim,
God hath in very deed appeared to plead

his own cause, and wipe away our reproach. To see young children walking the streets, early on Lord's day mornings before the sun beams covered them; and old men, walking every one with his staff in his hand for very age, was a sight, which angels must have seen with more than common transport.

Sixty were added to this church. These new members were from eleven to twenty years of age. A gradual work appeared in Camden, and twenty were added to the first church. Among the Freewillers many were brought to bow to the mild sceptre of Jesus, and adhere to him with full purpose of heart. In Hope, and in Lincolnville there has been a glorious display of God's astonishing grace.

> Great is the work my neighbours cri'd,
>   And own'd the power divine;
> Great is the work my heart reply'd,
>   And be the glory thine.

Mount Desert, Surry, Ellsworth, Trenton, and Sillivan have been visited with refreshing showers of mercy. Such displays of grace have never been witnessed in those regions since that country was settled. This revival appeared in 1816, and spread along the eastern banks of Penobscot River. The wilderness and the solitary place shall be glad for them : and the desert shall rejoice, and blossom as the rose. And of Eden, and of Columbia, and Addison, and Stueben, and Goldsborough, it shall be said, This and that man was born there.

His mercy visits every house,
That pay their night and morning vows;
But makes a more delightful stay,
Where churches meet to praise and pray.

BRUNSWICK, (Me.) 1818.
This work commenced in 1816, and Dr. Baldwin of Boston, was one very honoured

instrument in the all powerful hand of Jesus, in awakening the careless. He preached in a large hall, at 7 o'clock on the morning of July 22d, and about fifty were roused from spiritual slumber, and saw themselves verging towards infinite misery. The Saviour soon extended his hand, and delivered them from plunging into remediless ruin.

More than eighty were hopefully renovated, in the space of three weeks. At every meeting some came forward and told what the Lord had done for their souls. At one meeting, thirty related their experience, and as many more were desirous to come forward. What a wonderful work! Were Christians prepared to attend this exhibition of salvation, and receive converts daily into the churches? They truly were: for days of fasting and prayer were appointed, and strictly attended, for more than twelve months before, God came from Teman, and the Holy One from mount Paran. With pleasure they might hang upon

D

the prophets lips and say, His glory covered the heavens. and his brightness was
as the light; he had horns coming out of
his hand : and there was the hiding of his
power.

The ordinances were attended with an
unusual blessing to spectators, and the exhortations of young converts, were often
rendered powerful means of extending the
work, and refreshing the souls of old professors. The greatest regularity was pre-
served in all their meetings. Persons of
all ages, from nine to eighty years old have
been the happy subjects of this reformation. About three hundred have joined
themselves to the churches in this town.

Renew'd by grace, we love the word,
And yield our souls to Christ the Lord ;
Then to the church ourselves we give,
In holy fellowship to live.

BATH, (Me.) 1816.
The first favourable appearance, in this
place, that God was about to revive his

work, was an uncommon flocking to meetings, attended with a remarkable stillness and solemnity upon those who came. The Spirit seemed to descend like a mighty rushing wind, and soon a general attention prevailed through the town.

Each of the religious societies shared in the work. The means God has seen fit to honour, in spreading this work are many. A Methodist brother, in the more humble condition in life than multitudes, was apparently blest to the awakening of numbers. The appearance and conversation, of those who were brought out of darkness into God's marvellous light, carried conviction to the hearts of many.

Numbers went thoughtless to see the converts profess Jesus before men, but returned deeply impressed with a sense of their sin and danger. The preaching of Christ has been the power of God, and the wisdom of God to many, who walked in darkness, and saw no amiableness in Him who is altogether lovely, and the express image of the Father.

The aged, middle aged, and youth, have been enabled to come to Jesus. to cleanse them from sin. Some influential characters, and some in the lowest walks of life have been hopefully born of the Spirit. Among the young merchants, the work was so remarkable, that it was often said, that all the stores had become meeting houses. In the time of this revival, all have seemingly endeavoured to keep their passions within the bounds of reason. and only a few have made any noise that could disturb the most devout worshippers of the Lamb; and these were so e whelmed with a sense of their exposedness to endless punishment, that they groaned under the weight of their sins, and trembled at the thoughts of approaching judgment. Deep solemnity has generally marked the penitent; and a holy mile of joy and complacency, the pardoned sinner.

Since the beginning of this good work, about two hundred and fifty have been added to the churches in this town; which are Congregational, Baptist, and Methodist.

> To God, my Saviour and my king,
> Fain would my soul her tribute bring;
> Join me ye saints in songs of praise,
> For ye have known and felt his grace.

HEBRON, (Me.)

There were frequent appearances of a revival in this town, before it really quickened dead sinners, and caused them to follow Christ in the regeneration. A more than usual concern was manifested by professors, for a revival of religion. Meetings on Lord's days were full, and there seemed to be some attention to the word in time of worship; but no visible fruit appeared until the summer of 1816.—It was first reported that several youths were thought to be under serious concern for their souls. In September, a revival was apparent; some had found comfort to their minds, and others appeared anxiously concerned.

In October and November, the precious work kept increasing and spreading, till it was perceived in all parts of the society. December was a solemn and pleasing month. Prayer meetings were attended three times in a week, and sometimes oftener. These were much crowded, and the power of the Spirit was so manifested with the people, that there were but few, who were not awed with his presence. The young converts were made cheerfully to sing. while the eyes of the older Christians glistened with tears of joy, and others sighed under their worse than Egyptian bondage. The feelings of every one were more or less affected. The good news that this or that youth was under concern for his soul, or rejoicing in the love of God, daily awakened attention. Although their meetings were so crowded, and the attention so great, no disorder appeared; all was regular; only one spoke at a time, with the greatest calmness, and yet with

fervency. Reader, hast thou ever experienced this grace ? What are all the
splendours of the world, when compared
with the joy of such a season ?

This work has been principally among
the youths, and very few over thirty years
appear to have had a share in it. The subjects of it expressed a deep sense of their
vileness, and of the justice of God in their
condemnation, but not with a great deal
of terrour, as it respects positive future punishment. Their wretchedness was in themselves, and their hell in their own breasts.
They were soon brought to see, that they
must be holy or miserable, for ever. Generally when they received comfort, their
joy at first was but small, their views
faint, and their hope not more than pro-
portionable. In many instances they expressed a measure of delight in the Redeemer, when they hardly dared to hope
at all They gathered strength of mind
very gradually; but their trials seemed
more than usual, and it was some time be-

fore any of them were constrained, by the love of Christ, to make publick profession of his name. In January 1817, twenty, mostly youths, professed their faith In Christ. This was a solemn day, and long to be remembered with an holy pleasure. In February and March, a number more came forward and owned their Lord. About fifty in this town have been the hopeful subjects of regenerating influences.

His spirit did their tongues inspire,
And warm their hearts with heav'nly fire.

The District of Maine has been highly favoured of God. That region, a few years ago, contained only here and there a village, and a few towns skirting along the shores of the Atlantick. Now it is populous, rich and religion abounds among its inhabitants.

To the list of towns, of which we have read accounts unfolding God's free and unbounded compassion to sinners, we may add with much holy pleasure, Alfred, Waterborough, St. George, Nobleborough, Jefferson, Deerfield, Bowdoin, Sumner, Livermore, and Fayette. Upon these and many lying in their vicinity, the Spirit has descended, and its omnipotent energies have been experienced.

Not unto us, not unto us, but to thy name, O God! shall this glorious and gracious work be ascribed. Many whose heads are whitened with age, who have long borne the burden and heat of the day in the gospel vineyard, declare that never have such exhilarating tidings gladdened their hearts, nor such bright prospects met their eyes. Multitudes are now embosomed in the churches, who a few years since were roaming the wilds of nature, and speeding their way to the regions of blackness and unspeakable misery. May these converts all adorn the doctrine of God their Saviour, and finally sit down with the sanctified in the kingdom of heaven.

WOBURN, (Mass.)

This work first made its appearance in Lord's day evening conference meetings. Those were not statedly held until November 1816. They were first held in private houses, and but thinly attended. But thinly attended as they were, a resolution was formed among the Baptist brethren, not to forsake the assembling of themselves together, but to maintain these little meetings, so long as two or three would come. The meetings were maintained, and the number that attended them, instead of diminishing, gradually increased. Nor was it long before a disposition to converse and to hear, and a concern for the prosperity of souls, became manifest. A few Annas and Simeons, who had been long praying, and waiting for the consolation of Israel, now began to be revived, and fully convinced that prayer had been heard and answered, and that Jesus was at hand. Becoming zeal was manifest, in exhortations and prayers, especially in the latter.

Conference meetings began to be established in the congregational society, and the
number of anxious sinners fast increased ;
indeed, experimental religion began to be
generally considered, the one thing need-
fu'. The appearance of their religious assemblies was changed. It was such, as
plainly indicated that many were in their
imaginations, by a secret invisible impulse,
arraigned before the awful judgment seat
of Christ. Often did the steady, fixed
countenance, and the gently flowing tear,
forcibly express the contrition of the heart.
A spark, sometimes, falls, kindles and
spreads till the whole city is involved in
flames; so did the divine spark, which fell
in Woburn, kindle, burn, and spread, till
nearly the whole town was involved in one
sacred, gentle flame. Both societies and
persons of almost every age, have shared
in the work. Many have been constrained
to say, come and hear ye what the Lord
hath done for our souls. O come magnify
the Lord and let us exalt his name together.

In addition to other meetings, they held one weekly, particularly designed for serious inquiring sinners. These were found interesting and profitable. The number that attended was frequently, from twenty to forty. It is more easy to imagine, than to describe the feelings naturally excited on meeting with this number, most of them in tears, being under deep concern for their souls.

The relation, of candidates for admission to the church, have been clear and satisfactory. They expressed their full belief of their hearts being totally depraved, that none could change them but God, that Jesus Christ was a whole Saviour, and that all who were once united to him would be kept by his power through faith, unto salvation.

The additions made to both churches, in one year from the commencement of the revival, are nearly equal. The whole number is about 160.

Pawctucket (Mass.)

This revival began in the winter of 1815, and continued to progress almost two years. Additions were made to the church under the ministry of the Rev. Mr. Benedict, every month.

The subjects of this work have been of almost all ages, from twelve to upwards of sixty; most of them, however, are under the age of thirty. A large proportion of them are heads of families. A number of persons of considerable standing in society, who have heretofore looked with indifference or disdain on the religion of the heart, and have been building themselves up on good morals, or have been trusting in Universalism, Deism, or some other errors equally pernicious, have been brought to bow to the mild sceptre of the Redeemer, and have with cheerfulness, and delight, followed in his cross-bearing ways. One of the subjects of the revival was a singular instance of the invincible power of all-conquering grace. His life had been so

E

regular and upright, that the people all
around thought he was so good. that he
needed no change : and some, that he was
so wise, that he would not be taken with
this delusion.   And he himself, a few
months before his conversion, contended
strongly against the doctrine of the sinner's entire depravity of heart. and enmity
against God.   He considered 'it a high and
cruel charge, to accuse a sober and upright
man of being an enemy to his Maker, and
of hating and opposing him.   He appeared
sure that he had no such feelings, and
consequently felt no concern for the future.   Mr. Benedict conversed with him,
and felt much engaged for the salvation of
his soul : but all seemed to have no impression on the man.   Sometime after. he
took Mr. B. aside. and observed that his
views were altered—that he found he had
a wicked heart—that he owed a debt he
could never pay—that his mind was so
distressed he could do no business, and
knew not what to do; that he knew of

nothing in his conduct among mankind
which gave him trouble, but that the sins
of his heart were great and distressing,
and made him continually wretched and
miserable. After being a few weeks in
this distress, his deliverance was as joyful,
as his convictions had been severe. His
cup overflowed with joy. and in the Lord's
appointed ways he travelled forth with
composure and delight. May every one
who reads this, reflect on that man's condition, and experience the same heart
changing, and soul reviving influences.

The converts generally. have given very
clear and satisfactory accounts of their
conviction of sin. and of their being brought
to trust alone for salvation in the merits of
a crucified Redeemer. Though the work
has been remarkably still, yet in some instances. the tone of feeling has arisen high
in strains of joy and praise. One woman
was so transported in her feelings, and so
deeply impressed with the need of religion
for others, that she went out with a view

of informing her large circle of friends and relations, what a Saviour she had found. When she got into the street, she hardly knew how to spend time to go from one to another to tell them individually, but wanted some herald with a trumpet to sound it abroad, that they might all at once hear the glorious intelligence. Another was so enraptured with his views of the beauties of the Saviour, that he wanted to be on the house top, and have as many as could hear his voice, collected around him, that he might at once publish to them, the excellency of his glorious character. Amid this ardour of feeling, nothing like enthusiasm or reverie has at any time broke forth. No means were used, either to excite or restrain strong feelings and passions in the all important concerns of eternity; but many, to teach inquirers the odious nature of sin, and its ill deserts: believing that genuine conviction depends more on the views which the sinner has on these points, than the most frightful visions of death and eternity.

Since the commencement of this revival, more than one hundred were added to the Baptist church, a considerable number to the Episcopalians and some to the Methodists. In 1818 the work revived again, and some have been brought to rejoice in Christ, and many of the saints to a greater establishment in the plan of infinite benevolence.

ATTLEBOROUGH, (Mass.)

The Baptist church in this town being deprived of their minister by death, unanimously called the Rev. Stephen S. Nelson, to become their pastor. After many trials in his own mind, about leaving the people among whom he laboured, he finally concluded to accept of the invitation, and commenced his ministry among them in May, 1815. This connexion was sanctioned in heaven, and the Spirit descended in copious effusions.

E 2

The religious awakening spread rapidly from house to house, and from neighbourhood to neighbourhood, through this, and the adjacent towns. until the attention became general. Many of those who first came out, dated their impressions from the preaching of Mr. Nelson. before he moved among them. The Lord was there operating on the minds of many, before Mr. N. or the members of that church knew it.

This revival seemed to gather a multitude of young and old, of male and female, from nine to eighty years of age. Some vicious and abandoned, others more moral and pharisaical. One circumstance is here narrated worthy of transmitting down to posterity, and for the encouragement of bible institutions. A pious sister of this church was deeply impressed with the duty of presenting a bible to one of her poor, thoughtless and very stupid neighbours. She presented him one accompanied with an earnest request that he would.

frequently read it, and that God would bless and sanctify it to him, and his family for their spiritual and everlasting good. What said he to himself, can this mean? In what a condition does she view me, to make her so anxious for my salvation? How blind, how stupid and how hardened must I be, to know nothing of it myself? I will read this bible and see what these things mean. The more he read and reflected, the deeper his convictions grew, until he was hopefully converted.

This good work spread into the Congregational societies in this, and many other towns. Since its commencement, two hundred and fifty have professed to know Christ and the power of his resurrection. Of this number one hundred and twenty two have joined the Baptist church.

Providence, Warren, Bristol, Newport, Warweck, Exeter, and many other towns in that state have received gracious and very copious showers. Providence has been the most distinguished place for religious freedom, of any, within the boundary of our American Israel. On that spot, God has shed many drops of astonishing grace, and thousands have been purified for heaven. Some of the students in the University have been made alive to God. Within those walls prayer meetings have been multiplied, souls have been taught of Jesus, have entered a class for heaven, and have almost seen their names on that catalogue of happy beings, whose progress in theology shall continue with the revolutions of eternity.

> Lord when I count thy mercies o'er,
>   They strike me with surprise :
> Not all the sands that spread the shores
>   To equal numbers rise.

Thompson, Dudley, Killingly, Hampton, Pomfret, Woodstock, some parts of Ashford, Windham, Mansfield, and Coventry, (Conn.) have been visited from on high, and many souls quickened who were dead in trespasses and sins.

A particular account from each town cannot conveniently be admitted to occupy a place here as the revival began in many of them before 1815, but as the revival continued for about two years, it comes within my limits ; therefore, a few general remarks upon the whole, will be submitted for the entertainment of those, who love to gather up the fragments, that nothing be lost. The work that covered the above towns with mercy, began in the Rev. D. Dow's congregation. in November 1813. From this, it spread abroad, from conquering to conquer. The place, in which it appeared the most powerful, was a small factory village, denominated from its situation, the Swamp Factory. Here satan, for two or three years, seemed to reign with almost sovereign and despotick sway. His subjects who are generally very fond of dancing, here made great progress, and often kept their revelling meetings through the night.

A few pious souls lived in that Sodom.

These often prayed for their deluded neighbours. Their prayers were heard, and the spirit of grace descended upon the vilest of the vile. Conference meetings were held, and the servants of Christ came frequently and preached the word unto them, in power. These meetings were greatly blessed. Every heart seemed to know its own depravity, and to meditate upon the day of judgment Convictions were generally. of the most pungent and powerful kind. Some were arrested in a sudden manner : being one moment in the awful act of swearing, cursing, and ridiculing religion, and the next, calling on God to have mercy on their souls. Others, while in conference meetings which they attended to gratify their curiosity, or for the purpose of making observations, were in an instant made sensible of their desperate condition ; and very few who were thus arrested. ceased crying to God for mercy, until they had found pardon, and peace for their souls.

How changed the scene! Instead of the sound of the violin, the pounding motions of the feet. and the clamorous voices of drunkards and lewd wretches, the ears of the godly were saluted with songs of praise to God.

The scriptures were searched daily, especially by those, who were under conviction. Many of whom improved every moment they could spare, in perusing them and seemed determined, that nothing but the word of God should give them comfort. or direct the measures of their future conduct. Indeed, they ate with the bible in their hands, slept with it in their bosoms, and it seemed that all the world could not tempt them to part with this precious treasure. Many, after obtaining a good hope through grace, were disposed to unite with some church. One hundred and twelve joined the Baptist church in Thompson, and about one hundred and seventy to other churches. The number that professed Christ in the other towns, I have not obtained.

SUFFIELD, (Conn.)

This work commenced in the spring
1815, and progressed gradually through
the summer. In Autumn it became more
general and powerful.

The first instance of conversion, was a
young woman, who like many others had
been very careless and vain. Retiring to
rest one evening, as she blew out her can-
dle, the thought forcibly impressed her
mind, that God could as instantly blow
away her breath, and what then would become of her immortal soul. Her distress
was great, and her convictions increased,
until she was enabled to resign her all into
the hands of her blessed Saviour. She
related her experience and obeyed her
Lord. When she made this publick manifestation of her faith in him, and her de-
termination to walk in newness of life
with his professed friends, many of his
saints rejoiced, and some poor sinners were
pierced with the arrows of truth. From
this time the work extended its heavenly

flame, and the number of disciples increased in different parts of the town.

In December, it pleased him who must needs go through Samaria, to pass through the east street, where the people had remained unaffected and very indifferent about religion. He abode there more than two days, and made most wondrous displays of his power and mercy. The interesting realities of eternity were opened to their view, and the greatest part of the young people, together with many heads of families, through the street for three miles in length, have become the happy subjects of regeneration. A lad of twelve years, who had been a ringleader in vanity among his companions, obtained mercy, and was made instrumental of good to others in recommending the Saviour to many of his young friends. About the same time an aged man came forward trembling, and confessing that he had obtained a hope some years before, but had not lived accordingly, and that he now found him-

F

self a stumbling block in the way of others, and felt it his indispensable duty to leave this ground, and move forward in active obedience to his Lord's commands.

Many of different ages and stations in life have shared in this glorious work; yet the greatest number have been from among the youths.   To see a large number of young persons from ten to twenty years old, crowding the places of worship, to hear the precious word, or to hear them relating God's gracious dealings with their souls. singing praises to his name, and conversing on heavenly things, was truly affecting.   Nor was it less affecting to see some who had been valiant soldiers in the enemies' camp, yielding themselves the willing captives to victorious grace. About one hundred have joined the Baptist, and some the Congregational church in that place.

A cloud of witnesses around,
  Hold you in full survey;
Forget the steps already trod,
  And onward urge your way.

BRISTOL. (Conn.)

Previously to a revival in this place, great stupidity prevailed among all denominations of Christians, and those who had not been enroled among the followers of Jesus, were very negligent about attending the means of instruction. Some professors began to feel the real need of the quickening influences of the Holy Spirit. Prayer meetings were appointed and a few began to entreat the Lord to revive his work. The Spirit evidently interceded with their spirits, with that fervency that cannot be uttered. A general thoughtfulness began to occupy the minds of the people, whilst each one was ignorant of the impression made on others, and knew not but that his exercises were peculiar to himself.

Various causes served to expose the secret exercises of many, and increase the attention of the people. Preaching was accompanied with the power of God. Exhortations, and conversation, especially of renewed souls were greatly instrumental of good, and were as arrows made sharp in the hearts of the king's enemies. Meetings were held almost every day in the week. Great solemnity was apparent on the countenances of all, and many were heard to weep. Convictions were exceeding pungent, and in some few cases, natural strength being nearly overcome, limbs failed to perform their office as though unable to bear up the heavy load. Relief of mind has been generally attended with great joy.

The subjects of this work have been of every age from ten to eighty years. These have soon chosen, where they believed they could be the most useful and happy in church communion and fellowship. Sixty five joined the Congregationalists, sixty three the Baptist, and a considerable number the Methodist. Burlington, Plymouth, Wolcott, Southington, and Farmington have received abundance of grace, and multitudes have been turned from the evil of their ways, to serve the Lord and worship him in the beauty of holiness.

It would have been very gratifying to the writer, to have been able from correct documents, to have given the publick the numbers who have joined churches in the above towns: but he has obtained only general information. These will all appear in the day of judgment; for the Lord knoweth them that are his. No one shall be able to pluck them out of his hands. Who shall separate us, from the love of Christ?

MIDDLETOWN, (Conn.)

The work commenced about the middle of Jan. 1818, and continued until sometime in May. Previously to the commencement of this revival, it was truly a season of darkness; the ways of Zion mourned, and scarcely a fresh bud or blossom of grace appeared. It was truly a season cheerless and unpromising as winter itself. The

professed friends of Christ were generally
in a lukewarm state, possessing little zeal
either for the prosperity of the church. or
the salvation of souls. Only a few seemed
to long and pray for a revival of religion,
and even these few were often discouraged
and ready to faint. Sermons, exhortations, and prayers, apparently produced
no effect; many of the saints slumbered
and sinners slept upon the brink of ruin.

About this time, it pleased God to pour
out his Spirit upon the people in the north
parish. The work was powerful and spread
rapidly through that society. In less than
a month, great numbers were made deeply sensible of their sinfulness, and were
led to inquire anxiously, what they must
do to be saved. Several by this time had
obtained a hope of eternal life through
the merits of the Lamb, and rejoiced believing with all their hearts.

Soon after this revival commenced, the
Rev. Mr. Jinks observes, that he began to
hope that God would visit the people of

his charge with a gracious shower. Under this impression, he appointed meetings more frequently, which were better attended than formerly. Yet nothing special appeared to take place for some time. The Rev. Mr. Graves and Brigis preached frequently in a school house at Millers' farms with like expectations; but such was the hardness of the hearts, and the stupidity that attended that people, that only a few were disposed to hear any preacher.

Nearly a month elapsed since the work began in the north parish, and the people of the south appearing so indifferent about their future state, that Mr. J. began to fear that God was about to give up his people to the plague of their own hearts and leave them to their own chosen way. This conclusion was strengthened by a circumstance that took place on a Lord's day somewhat unfavourable as to the weather. Only six or seven beside those who resided in his house attended meeting. This may show how very careless that people were; for the city of Middletown contains as many inhabitants as any other of the same number of houses in the New-England states. It would be vain to give a description of his feelings on that day. He retired home with a heavy heart, and all his fond hopes that God would revive his work in that place. vanished away like the early dew, and all his expectations were cut off. He now concluded that God did not call him to preach to a people, that had no relish for the word of life, and that it was his duty to leave them, and proclaim the glad tidings of the gospel to those who were perishing for lack of knowledge. and would be more ready to hear that their souls might live. This, however, was the last watch of the night. The sun of righteousness was about to arise, and by the brightness of his coming, to dispel the darkness that had so long hung over them.

These circumstances are noticed, not

out of any disrespect to that people, but
with a view that others may not be dis-
heartened in the darkest season : For the
ways of God are past finding out, and the
darkest appearances, of his providence,
are often the sure tokens of a bright and
glorious morning.

In such dark seasons of rebuke and
trial, God usually humbles and prepares
his people to receive the greatest blessings.
God will not hide his cheering countenance from any people beyond the set time
to favour them, and glorify his rich grace,
in comforting those who wait for his salvation. This was most strikingly evidenc-
ed in Middletown. For, the very Tuesday after Mr. J's. trials on the Sabbath, as
he was passing a Mr. Johnson's factory
within the bounds of his society, he felt an
inclination to call, though he had no business to transact. On entering, he found
not the owner within, and was about to
leave, but one of the workmen with whom
he had been acquainted, seemed desirious

to speak with him.   He went unto him and entered into conversation.   This workman began immediately to give a relation of the exercises of his mind, and without hesitation, and without being asked; he said, that he found himself, to be a poor, lost, and ruined sinner : that he had been greatly distressed on this account, two or three weeks, and that he knew not what to do. He also observed, that one of his shopmates saw himself in the same condition, and was in much distress of mind.

Mr. Jinks was so astonished in hearing this man converse, that for a moment he was unable to make any reply. He now saw clearly that he had been limiting the power of the Holy One of Israel, and distrusting his goodness.   In a moment, hope revived, and faith triumphed over unbelief; the fears, gloom and darkness that had distressed his mind for three days past, now fled away, like the shadows of night before the rising sun.   He now had conclusive evidence, that God had begun a revival of religion, and even in a place, where he had not so much as thought, that one would be taken. An indescribable change instantly took place in his mind. He was comforted, and strengthened, and began to attend meetings fully convinced that he was about to see a rich harvest of souls. Suitable texts were easily found, and words to elucidate them, which flowed not in vain. Christians generally began to feel the effects of a gracious visitation. Their meetings were more frequent, full, solemn, and interesting.

It was astonishing to see the change that took place in two weeks. Saints were filled with transports of joy, and sinners were pricked in their heart and began anxiously to inquire what they must do to be saved. Hundreds flocked to places of worship. The darkest nights, the most unfavourable weather, and unpleasant travelling did not hinder their assembling together. Though there were meetings every night in the week, yet these were so crowded, that many had to stand at the doors, and windows, in order to hear the word of life, and some had to go away who could not get near enough to hear. Many of the young people who had been vain and thoughtless about eternity, were now seen with their heads bowed down, and trembling with fear, lest the mercies of God were clean gone for ever. The hearts of some of the most obdurate sinners seemed to melt like wax before the fire, and many who once would not have been thought to be serious, for the greatest consideration, were now constrained to renounce their sinful ways, to cry unto God for salvation, and to beseech Christians to pray for them This good work increased with great rapidity, and about an hundred in a few weeks were convinced that they must be born again, or die in their sins. Their distress was generally great. During the first part of their exercises, they wept much, but as the work progressed in their hearts, their tears subsided, and they felt such a sense of their great depravity and sinfulness, that they trembled at the thought of approaching the judgment seat of Christ. Most of the subjects of this work, appeared to have a deep sense of the evil of sin, and to feel in the latter part of their convictions, that they had a heart opposed to God and full of enmity against him. Some felt ready to conclude, that he was neither just nor merciful: but when they were brought to see their helplessness and deserved punishment for sin, they were constrained to acknowledge the justice of God, in their final condemnation, and had clear views of justification alone, through the righteousness of Christ.

There was now great joy in that city and the region around. Parents were often seen rejoicing over a son, or daughter, who had been hopefully made a subject of grace. Brothers and sisters often mingled their tears, weeping at the joyful recollection of what the Lord had recently done for their souls. Young converts often went

G

from house to house, to tell what they had
experienced, and to warn their companions
to flee from the wrath to come. In many
instances, their exhortations produced the
desired effect. and were the means of convincing some of the danger of living and
dying in a state of impenitence.

In some families God wrought wonders
of divine grace. In one family the last
member, a son, who had long slighted the
Saviour, was brought to know him and the
riches of his grace: in another, both parents and three of their children were made
the hopeful subjects of a saving change in
less than a year. In five families both
husbands and wives became the humble
followers of Christ, and rejoiced in hope
of the glory of God.

This work continued about three months,
in which time, not less than one hundred
and thirty appeared to have experienced
the renovating influences of the Spirit.
Among this number. some with great propriety may be stiled *brands plucked out of*

the burning. These profane sinners, have become exemplary followers of Christ. Many youths, who were sporting along the road of life, unconscious of danger, have been stopped in their thoughtless career, and become humble penitents. The greatest number, who have professed Christ in this revival, are under twenty five years. Not one is known in Mr. Jinks' society, as being a subject of this work who is above fifty years old.

Reader, art thou young? Let this be a warning to thee, not to put off repentance until old age. It may then be too late.—Now is the accepted time, and now is the day of salvation.

This work spread among the Baptist and Methodist denominations and many were added to them. As this work was of God, he saw fit to commence it, when it seemed best in his great plan, and to use such instruments as should redown most to his glory when he should make up his jewels.

Several ministers, doubtless have been honoured of God in their labours in that region, who will in the great day appear with these souls to add lustre to their crowns of rejoicing.

Most of those who obtained hopes in this reformation, adorn the doctrine of God our Saviour, by a well ordered life and conversation. Those who have fallen away from their professions, are persons whose convictions were generally short: and who did neither know the sinfulness of their own hearts. nor the powerful merits of Christ's atoning bloo '

The number added to the churches in the north part of this town, the compiler has not received. In Rocky Hill a revival began last season, and many souls were brought to love our Lord supremely. Haddam has likewise received a rich manifestation of grace, and many towns along the Connecticut River, and some bordering on the sea; as Guilford, Brandford, and the city of New-Haven. The College in that city caught a few drops of mercy from heaven, and some young men who went thither to become eminent in human science, have become wise unto salvation. May they be burning and shining lights in the world, and be instrumental of turning many to righteousness.

Once more, we may turn our attention up the Connecticut River. There we behold the city of Hartford, as a most distinguished place in the catalogue of towns exalted to heaven, in privileges and appearing before the throne with a multitude of converts. Within a few years, the churches have been so constantly favoured with refreshing streams of salvation, and large additions of members, that they seem to view these manifestations so common, that they have neglected to give information to the world that the Lord is among them of a truth. East-Hartford has been extensively revived. Windsor has been alarmed, and a few have fled for refuge and laid hold on the hope set before them

G 2

in the gospel. Enfield has been remembered before God, and some have left their all and followed Jesus. Suffield has been noticed, as sharing largely in tha: mercy which endureth for ever. Over East-Springfield the cloud passed, only distiling as it passed here and there a reviving drop. Over West-Springfield it hung for many days. The thunder of God's power was heard, rockey hearts rent, the graves of sinners were opened and many of the saints arose Blessed be God, they did not wish to sleep any longer among the dead, for their salvation was nearer than when they believed. They held from seven to ten meetings in a week. The people flocked to these meetings with willing minds and large numbers were made acquainted with the Saviour of sinners. All denominations shared in this soul ravishing, and saving work. About fifty joined the Baptist church under the ministry of the Rev. Mr. Rand, and many the Presbyterian church.

The Spirit came down like a copious

shower on Hadley. North Hampton, Hatfield, Deerfield, Sunderland, Montague, Leverett, and a large number of towns in the vicinity of these, and many hundreds were added to the Congregational churches; and other denominations who hold the principles of the doctrine of Christ, had considerable additions. The Spirit continued to spread its amazing, and heart reviving influences for more than two hundred miles into the northern regions. To give only a brief narrative of the means and instruments which God honoured; the views which many had, when the work began to appear among them; the prayer meetings, humbling seasons, and joys that the followers of Jesus had; the anxiety, sorrows and almost distressing terrours, which sinners felt; the multitudes, of different ages, sexes, conditions, characters, and complexions, who finally professed to have left Egyptian slavery, crossed the Red sea and begun their journey towards a better country, would fill many volumes.

Yet some events were so interesting that the writer cannot think himself justified in passing them by, when the towns in which they took place. are mentioned. In Putney, a part of Brattleborough, Westminster, Westmoreland, and Keene, God has wrought wonderfully.

ALSTEAD, (N. H.)

The work first appeared in a small village in the west part of this town in Dec. 1814. From this part it spread and touched upon some of the borders of Walpole.

A small number of professors met on Lord's day evenings for religious conference, which they continued under many discouraging circumstances, hoping, though with much trembling, that they should see the glory of God. At one of these meetings, a man about forty years happened to be present, who on his return home, began to inquire in himself, what it could be that should induce these people to meet together? It seemed as though, an agent unseen by the natural eye was operating on his mind, and said to his soul, that it was religion; and that this religion was a divine reality, and that he was destitute of it. This text was brought powerfully to his mind. *Thou fool, this night thy soul shall be required of thee!* His sins were set in order before him, and a deep sense of God's justice in his condemnation, which filled his soul with unspeakable anguish and distress. But the Lord soon appeared for him, and gave him joy and peace in believing. At the next conference, he came forward and declared what God had done for his soul to the astonishment of all present. Many soon came in to hear, and a number became impressed, and the work began.

Those who first experienced renovating grace were heads of families, who had past the meridian of life, and some had arrived to old age. In the spring of 1815, the work spread among the young people. This was quick and powerful. The attention, of many was suddenly arrested without any extraordinary means, and in about four days. the most of them were rejoicing in the God of their salvation. All unnecessary business was suspended, and the place seemed,

A young heaven on earthly ground,
And glory in the bud.

The change produced by this work is very apparent. In those families where God was not worshipped. there the evening and morning prayers now ascend towards heaven. Those who rarely. if ever attended publick worship, are now constantly attentive to the duties of the sanctuary. Those youths who were over fond of carnal diversions, now view them with abhorrence. and appear much more delighted in meeting for prayer and religious conference.

The special agency of the divine Spirit has been remarkably manifested in this revival. Ordinary means and instruments seemed almost entirely excluded. If any have been rendered important and crowned with success, they have been principally the subjects of the work. Paul may plant and an Apollos water, but God must give the increase.

Distinguishing grace has been marvellously displayed in the choice of those, who have been the subjects of this glorious work. Some of all ages and classes, from twelve to about seventy years, have been called. The most of them had treated, even the common forms of religious instruction, with neglect. and some had held the whole in the highest contempt. They are justly viewed as brands plucked out of the fire.

Amazing goodness! love divine!
O may our grateful hearts adore
The matchless grace, nor yield to sin
Nor wear its cruel fetters more!

ROCKINGHAM, (Vt.)

The work in this and some of the towns in its vicinity has been truly gracious, and occasioned unspeakable joy to Christians. Many have felt the power of the Spirit and have been enabled to fly to Jesus for salvation. Large accessions have been made to the churches. The small church over which the Rev. Mr. Elliot was settled, a few years since, has become numerous, and the meeting house filled with attentive hearers. The good work appeared glorious in Cornish (N. H.) Multitudes of men, women, and children have experienced the grace of God. Meetings, in every part of that town, were held daily, for many months. An almost universal attention was paid to these, by its inhabitants. People from the neighbouring towns would frequently go over to see and hear what wonderful things the converts could exhibit to gratify their curiosity. Some who came to mock, retired with deep wounds in their hearts. From Cornish the work extended to other places. Plainfield was considerably refreshed. and a number have professed Jesus before men. Windsor received a few rich drops of mercy, from that cloud of righteousness, that seemed to contain the thunder of God's power, and abundance of the water of life, for thirsting multitudes.

While the Spirit moved upon the hearts of hundreds in Cornish, the people in Windsor appeared unconcerned and given over to frolick along the broad road to hell. On one side of the Connecticut River, all seemed engaged in religion ; on the other, all engaged after wordly emoluments, honours and amusements. A few Christians saw the signs of the times, and began to pour out their petitions before the throne of heaven, and to beseech the Lord Jesus to come, and tarry, and make known his power in Windsor. *His ear was not heavy nor his arm shortened.* Meetings began to multiply, and sinners began to hear the word with greater solemnity. The peals of Sinai's thunder fell, and souls began to

H

see and feel themselves in danger of hell
fire. The deluded sons and daughters of
pleasure, sought with all possible subtility
to maintain their balls and associations of
amusing foolishness, but found themselves
disappointed and overwhelmed with confusion. The revival gradually advanced,
sinners were alarmed, and Christians greatly engaged in prayer and exhortation. The
writer being pastor of a church in that
village, was eye, and he hopes heart witness to some influences of the spirit upon
that place. One day he visited a family
of his charge, of whom it was said, that
the Spirit had awakened: He found the
report verified. On arriving at the door,
the man of the house met him, with the
bible open, and tears rolling down his
cheeks. His heart seemed so full of distress, that he struggled sometime before
he could utter a single sentence. After
his passions were a little reduced, he began to relate what his views, sentiments
and manner of life had been; and what he
now felt and believed. He said that in

the morning of life he was often thoughtful
and very seriously inclined; but towards
the meridian of life he embraced the sentiments of the Universalists and became
very careless. He was lately brought to
a sense of his wretched condition, and
very frequently thought that his sentiments
were so abhorrent in God's sight, that pardon could not consistently be granted him
—that he viewed himself to be the chief
of sinners—that God would be just in ut-
tering that awful sentence against him,
*Depart ye cursed into everlasting fire, pre-
pared for the devil and his angels.* The
agony of his soul appeared to be inexpressible. He walked, and wept and frequently, would say, I am ruined for ever; my
sins are too great to be forgiven.

This was an house of sorrow, and of joy.
His wife and a daughter of about fourteen,
had obtained comfort in believing in Jesus:
another daughter and son declared that
they were under condemnation, and that
the wrath of God was upon them. This
scene was soon changed. The man was

brought to cast himself at the feet of Jesus, and had very clear views of his rich, free and unspeakable grace; and that God could be just. and yet through the merits of Christ, could consistently pardon. even such an hell deserving sinner as himself. Joy beamed in his countenance. He appeared anxious to let every one know whom he met, that Jesus was precious and could save unto the uttermost all who come unto God by him. His daughter who was deeply concerned, had also obtained hope. These four in one family, and 'en of other families related their experiences to the church of which the writer was pastor, and professed their faith in Christ on the 5th May 1816. Hundreds assembled on this occasion, and from the solemnity of their countenances. and the flowing tears that often bathed their cheeks, we might almost conclude that they were constrained to say within themselves, this religion must appear important to these converts; it must possess powerful charms, and singular influences to make them appear so happy, so heavenly, and so willing to leave us all, for Christ. Some among the crowd knew by experience, that the religion these professed, was the *One thing needful ;* and some had impressions made on their minds, that will be remembered in the day of judgment.

Two other circumstances are worthy of divulgation. A number of rude young men were determined to hold on their way in vanity, and not to regard the Lord's day, nor attend its solemn assemblies, nor hear what the ministers of Jesus had to deliver in their masters name. These chose a room in a printing office in which a number of them usually laboured, and to fasten their attention, and entertain their depraved souls, they commenced card playing. This they continued so long that one arose to walk across the room to rest himself ; in passing by a table or shelf he saw the bible lie open ; he stepped up and thought that he would amuse his mind for a moment in looking into that. The first passage in those blessed pages that caught his eye

H 2

was this, *Except ye repent, ye shall all
likewise perish.* He gazed upon the passage with astonishment, and read it over
again—*Except ye repent, ye shall all likewise perish.* I believe the declaration, said
the young man to himself, and I must perish
in my sins, unless there is some way for
my escape, that I have never yet known.
His soul was filled with distress, he left
the room and his wicked companions, and
sought to find a place, in God's earthly
sanctuary. Card playing, dancing and every
other vain, and soul destroying amusement
was left. No place, but that in which Jesus
was preached, in which his saints prayed,
sung and exhorted could now be desired by
him. His concern continued a few weeks,
and Christ we hope gave him rest. Another
youth of a similar disposition and practice
was arrested one evening, as he was retiring to bed at a late hour of the night,
found all the beds in the room apparently
full, and turning himself about said, and
where shall I lodge ? This being a tavern,
a traveller had taken the bed in which this

young man usually slept; and thanks for
ever be rendered unto God, for stopping
one of his servants to rest in that house, and
for directing him to that very bed. This
pious man said, come and sleep with me.
He accepted the invitation. The traveller ventured to ask him a few questions.
Are you a young gentleman of wealth? No
sir, replied the young man. What would
you give for a ticket, if you could have assurance, that it would draw a prize high
enough for your comfortable subsistence
while you lived? I would give any thing I
now possess and should be willing to labour
a number of months to obtain such a ticket.
Would you give all you have to be entitled
to a kingdom, and be assured that in a very
short time, you should enter it and possess
it. O Sir, that is carrying things to far,
there is no kingdom to be obtained by poor
persons in this way. Yes young man. there
is the kingdom of heaven. *Blessed are the
poor in spirit, for theirs is the kingdom of
heaven. Ask and you shall receive. And
whatsoever ye shall ask in my name, that*

*will **I** do*, said Jesus. *And **I** appoint unto you a kingdom. Seek first the kingdom of heaven.* You can have this kingdom, young man, through the merits of Christ, only for asking. This kingdom will never fade away, it will never be destroyed.

The traveller fell asleep, and the young man pondered upon what had been said. After meditating sometime upon the theme of their conversation he slept until morning. When he awoke, the man was gone on his way, but what he had said remained fixed in his soul. *Ask and you shall receive a kingdom* rung in his ears. All his vain associates who saw him the next day, discovered a change in his countenance. He could no longer jest and be merry in their presence. He could no longer mingle in the crowd of thoughtless sinners and squander away his precious time in recreations. The thunder of Sinai reached his ears, and flaming justice spread around him. *There is no peace, saith the Lord, unto the wicked.* This seemed for some time to hang heavy on his soul. He and many young persons were hopefully converted in this revival.

Hartland shared in this work. Norwick had a very refreshing shower. Many souls were brought home to God. Lebanon experienced some mercy drops Hanover was highly favoured, especially in the north east part of the town. Large numbers were awakened, and a considerable number were made alive to God, and united with the churches in that region. The writer is happy, in having it in his power to inform the publick that the College, from which, many pious young men have come forth to preach Jesus, and have been very eminent in the ministry, was not passed by. On that distinguished seat of literature, the Spirit made known its omnipotent energies. Some who came to that place, with hearts of entire selfishness, felt in the time of this revival the expanding influences of grace, and were made willing to *count all things, but loss for the excellency of the knowledge of Christ Jesus.* This grace rendered them very active for God and the souls of their fellow men. They held prayer meetings, appointed conferences, and went out into different parts of that town, and into the village of Norwick, and exhorted sinners to repent, and saints *to awake, and arise from the dead.* God owned their labours and added to their numbers.

The writer had the pleasure of attending two of those meetings, and can with much satisfaction announce, that those seasons are yet recollected with more than ordinary gratitude to our ascended Redeemer, who gave gifts to those students, and dispositions fervently engaged for the salvation of men, and the glory of Christ.

This work extended far up the River and spread wide into both states. Vermont has been partially blessed with revivals for many years: but in 1816 the heavens seemed to bow down upon her thousand summits, and the Spirit spread its effusions into more than one hundred societies. The work was most remarkable and illustrious. From some of the towns I have obtained very accurate narratives, and shall present them to my readers : fully believing that the same spirit that descended upon those thousands, will descend upon some who may peruse these refreshing accounts.

> Your harps, ye trembling saints,
>   Down from the willows take ;
> Loud to the praise of Christ our Lord,
>   Bid every string awake.

FAIR-HAVEN.

The church of which the Rev. R. Cushman was pastor, had become very small. Only four males, and twenty five females were members in August 1816. During the whole of the summer a dark cloud overspread them, and the frowns of divine Providence were generally felt in all parts of New-England. Mr. Cushman, and many more of his people than he expected assembled on the 31st July, agreeably to his request, and spent the day in fasting, humiliation, and prayer. From that time his meetings on Lord's days began to be more full and more solemn.

About the first of September, the Rev. Mr. Beaman of the State of Georgia preach- ed for Mr. Cushman a number of times. Being uncommonly gifted in oratory, he drew together a multitude of hearers, from all quarters. The Holy Spirit attended his preaching, and he was peculiarly faith- ful to his Master, and the souls of his hear- ers. He was evidently made an instru- ment in the hand of God, of great good to that people, by exciting general attention to the subject of religion, which began to be a general topick of conversation in al- most every circle. Besides this general attention and solemnity, nothing special appeared as yet, excepting in Mr. Cush- man's feelings. He began to be sensibly impressed with the almost certainty, that God was about to pour out his Spirit and effect a general reformation. It appeared, as though, he could see the cloud gather, and the showers of divine grace approach. He felt prepared, and stood ready to at-

tend to whatever God had for him to do in
such a work, in a different sense from what
he ever did before. Though he had always
been wishing, and praying for such a season, yet he never felt to stand in a waiting
posture till then.

Although the peculiarly melancholy season, and the powerful preaching of Mr. B.
were undoubtedly the means, in the hand
of God, of exciting general attention; yet
there were other instruments, which con-
spired to aid on the glorious work. About
the first of September, conference meetings, which had been entirely neglected
during the summer, were again revived.
The first meeting was well attended and
solemn. Among those who attended, was
a man, about forty five, who had always
been a leading character, and doubtless
had more influence in the town and society,
than any other individual. He was not
only forward in town affairs, in erecting
an elegant house for publick worship, in
supporting the gospel, and in all useful
publick institutions; but was also a leader

I

in all publick celebrations, and vain diversions. He was a punctual attendant upon publick worship; but seldom attended conference. Being only a few professors present, Mr. Cushman asked him, if he had nothing to say. He rose immediately, and addressed the assembly, directing his conversation particularly to the young people. He told them that he had lately been to Granville, (N. Y) where there was a revival; and he found the people engaged in things of religion. The attention, he observed was not confined to women and children, and men of weak minds: but men of the first characters, and talents, were engaged, and spent considerable of their time in attending meetings, and persuading their fellow sinners to repent. He seemed to talk as though he had doubts respecting the divinity of the scriptures, and the truth of religion. But said that there might be a reality in these things, as so many were engaged in them; and if so, it was all important for them to know it. And as they never could have a better op-

portunity, he advised them to give up their
diversions and vain amusements, for the
present, and devote the fall and winter to
the examination of the subject. He said
he would unite with them, and make a
thorough inquiry. If after a faithful, impartial and thorough examination, they
should find that religion was a farce, heaven
an imaginary good, and hell a bug-bear,
they would give themselves no more trouble
about it. But if they found those things
to be realities, as many of superiour talents
and solemnly believe, they must be all important; and they would give all diligence
to obtain an interest in them. If they were
important to one, they were to all. And
if they were any thing, they were every
thing.

The people heard with attention; and
by their profound silence, seemed to yield
their assent, and enter into the solemn
agreement. It was then proposed to attend to a number of questions which were
calculated to lead the mind to inquire into
the reality and importance of religion. A

question was accordingly proposed to be discussed the next Lord's day evening, respecting the immortality of the soul. The next, man's accountability. The truth of the scriptures, future state of retribution, &c. By the time these questions were discussed, many, who attended, were convinced that religion indeed was a reality, and of the first importance. They found, that it was high time to attend to the concerns of eternity, and secure the salvation of their immortal souls. Their meetings increased, and were more and more interesting and solemn.

Towards the end of September cases of conviction began to multiply. God was evide tl among the by the powerful operations of his Spirit. Conferences were appointed in different neighbourhoods, and were generally crowded : but there were no hopeful conversions till about the first of November. As the man above mentioned had always gone forward, and taken the lead in all their affairs and diversions, and had made the proposal to attend to the things of religion; it seemed as though the people were then waiting for him to break the way, and lead them into the kingdom of heaven. Though he was much engaged, continually going from house to house, persuading sinners to attend meetings, and seek their soul's salvation, and was under solemn conviction of his own lost state by nature; yet his heart seemed to resist, for a long time the influences of the Spirit. His conviction increased, and his anxiety for the salvation of his neighbours did not abate. At a conference in the meeting house on the first Lord's day in November, he was much distressed, related the exercises of his own mind, expressed a sense of his own perilous situation, and warned the people. Towards the close of the meeting he rose again and spoke at considerable length, and in such a manner as to interest the feelings, and gain the uncommon attention of the whole audience. He then mentioned the solemn resolution that he had made; that he was determined, by the strength of the Almighty, to seek an interest in Christ, make religion his business and serve his God the remainder of his days. He urged it upon all the people to make the same resolution, and used many impressive arguments. When he had gotten their minds wrought up to an high pitch, he made a proposal to them, and earnestly requested that all those who had any regard for their own souls, and were willing to make such a resolution, would then manifest it by falling upon their knees with him, and saying the Lord's prayer. It being so sudden, and unexpected, the whole assembly were struck and seemed to drop at once. Many, if not the greatest part at that moment, made the solemn resolve; and pledged themselves to fulfil, by the repetition of those sacred words. When they came to reflect upon the transaction which was done by many without any premeditation, being thus called to it unawares, they were so struck with their high obligations to God, that they could find no rest to their souls till they had paid their vow, and by the

Spirit had cordially embraced the Lord Jesus Christ.

A number, though somewhat impressed before, dated their first deep concern for their souls from this meeting and from their sudden resolution. The man who called the people to the resolution, himself, seeing the immediate effect, was also struck with a more awful sense of his own situation. He saw that it was likely that God was making an instrument of him, to call up the attention of the people to the concerns of eternity: and it struck his mind with force, that he might be the means of the conviction and conversion of some sinners; and while they were delivered from destruction, by his instrumentality, he himself should be cast down to hell. He was not alone in his fears. His own publick, and solemn resolution also, seemed to heighten his distress and increase his conviction. His anxiety was so great after this transaction, that he scarcely closed his eyes to sleep that night. He went from the meeting to his own house, but could not retire to rest from a sense of his awful situation. He went out to one of his neighbours whose wife was pious, and the only professor living in the village, and requested her to pray for him. The husband and two workmen were present, and under deep distress for their own souls. She told him that he must pray for himself. He said, he was so wicked he could not pray. She urged it upon him again and again. He finally concluded, that, if she would pray for him, that he might pray, he would make the attempt: for they all felt as though they must have a prayer, and there was no other professor near. Accordingly, they all kneeled down and he attempted to pray—but received no relief. He said afterwards, that his heart appeared as hard as a stone, and his prayer, like that in the meeting house, seemed not to rise above his head. God appeared at a vast distance; and it was with the greatest difficulty that he could bring him into his mind. He scarcely knew what he wanted in prayer, and it seemed to him all abomination. He then returned home, and continued in the same frame of mind all night and the next day. Sleep and rest departed from him. Monday evening was the stated time of their weekly prayer meeting, and it was held at his house by the request of his wife. Many attended, and the meeting was solemn and interesting. He was more calm in his mind during the services; and that night he rested quietly until morning. When he awoke he found a surprising alteration in his feelings. God appeared near to him, and he felt reconciled to him through Jesus Christ, whom he could then clearly see as he said on the right hand of the Father interceding for his people. Before this time he never had such a clear view of the Saviour, as mediator between God and man. He seemed to embrace him and trust in his merits alone for salvation.

Before the revival commenced, there was not a male professor in the village, and but very few in town. When the minds of the people began to be called up to the concerns of eternity, and their consciences awakened. they began to see their desolation, and feel the propriety and importance of family prayer. But as none could pray, or dare make the attempt, this man proposed to have as many as could attend, meet every morning in the schoolhouse at seven o'clock, and have Mr. Cushman go and read a chapter in the bible and pray with them as a substitute for family prayers in their own houses. This practice was continued from the commencement of the revival, till they began to pray in their own families. These meetings were owned of God, and blessed to the good of many souls.

This man said on Tuesday morning at their prayer meeting, that he felt as though he could submit to God. About the same time a number were brought into the kingdom. How wonderful are the ways of God! Though he is infinitely able to bring people to experience his grace, without means as well as with; yet he always uses them, and just such as he pleases, as though he could do nothing without; and often in a manner surprising to us, but always honourable to himself.

Immediately after the conversion of the man who had been so instrumental in calling up the attention of others, the work rapidly increased. Every day for some weeks, there were some instances of conviction, and some hopeful conversions. These converts were humble, and solemn, and alive in the cause of religion. That man, in a special manner of whom considerable has already been written, dwelt upon a theme entirely new. He was the first, who made a profession of his faith in Christ.

In November and December the work of God was so powerful, and made such wonderful progress, that all apparent opposition was hushed; and it appeared that all were coming and would bow before the all-conquering Spirit of grace, to the mild sceptre of the Prince of Peace. All was unity and love among Christians. The principal inquiry among the impenitent, was, *What shall we do to be saved?* The converts seemed to think of little else, but to glorify God their Deliverer, and do something to advance his cause, and persuade their fellow beings to be reconciled to God, through the merits of Christ.

Though this account has already been drawn out to a greater length than many others, yet the writer persuades himself, that his readers will be still entertained, with the relation of a few more cases, in which the agency of the Spirit is most illustriously made known.

One man, nearly sixty, who had been an influential character, and forward in supporting the gospel, and other useful institutions, but far from religion, was unexpectedly wrought upon by the Spirit of God and made a hopeful subject of his special grace. He was a man of undoubted veracity and strict integrity. He had the confidence of the publick and discharged the duties of several offices of trust in the town with faithfulness and ability. He was generally considered moral, though not entirely free from profanity. He was a warm friend, but a severe enemy. He was perhaps, in the strictest sense one of those who loved his friends and hated his enemies, and considered himself justified in so doing. He had been a violent opposer of the doctrine of grace; but finding that he could not maintain an argument against it, he became in a measure convinced of his errour, and showed no publick opposition to the doctrine for some years. He generally attended publick worship; and depended for salvation upon his own works. He thought if he were moral in his external conduct, he should certainly be saved. He had a long catalogue of supposed good works, set to his account, which he confidently believed would more than balance all the charges which God might have against him; and with these he expected to purchase salvation. Upon this ground he was so firmly fixed that he could not be driven from it by all the arguments which could be drawn from reason and the word of God. He knew the mind of clear and

K

well doctrinated Christians respecting him, and was sensible that the preaching which he constantly heard was all against him. But all did not avail any thing to alter his opinion respecting himself. He was ignorant of the Scriptures, having turned his attention almost wholly to things of a worldly nature. He often addressed the people at conference meetings. He besought them to reform, and become religious, and be engaged; and he said, he meant to be as religious as any of them; having no idea of the depravity of his own heart, or necessity of a change; but supposed, that all that was necessary to be religious, was to be morally honest, punctual in performing some external duties, and a certain degree of engagedness in the cause. And all this might be done, with such hearts as they already had. Mr. Cushman had often conversed with him upon this subject. endeavouring to show him his true situation, the danger of resting upon such ground, and the importance of regeneration; but apparently to very little effect.

He called upon Mr. Cushman one day, and conversed upon what Mr. C. had often urged upon his hearers concerning self-examination, and how if hearers would be faithful to themselves they might assertain the state of their hearts; and that he had according to those directions, made a faithful, and thorough examination, and found that his heart was changed, if this were necessary; it was certainly right at last; for he had done many things to the glory of God. With a degree of surprise Mr. C. said, Well, I am more discouraged. Upon which the man raised his voice and said, Why? What other motive could I have in entertaining and supporting ministers, building meeting houses, attending meetings, relieving the distressed &c.? Mr. C. viewed it of no importance to converse much with him; for the man was still fixed in selfishness, and came to establish his own righteousness. This reluctance to converse with him considerably agitated his mind. Mr. C. perceiving this, and the apparent anxiety of his mind, and that he was not entirely easy and secure, conversed freely and dealt plainly with him. The man listened with attention, and was somewhat affected.

Some days after this conversation, he knowing the opinion of his minister, and many Christians concerning him, he determined to sit down, and try the solidity and strength of his foundation for future happiness. He accordingly recounted over deliberately and reckoned up his good deeds, which he had been placing to his credit for so many years : and found as he thought, that they were so numerous and of so good a quality that a just God could not send him to hell. His mountain then stood stronger than ever : but the thought recurred to his mind, that he might have some evil deeds and he would add them up also, compare them with his good works, and strike the balance. He accordingly began to reckon them up, one by one, and soon found that they were more numerous than what he had ever imagined. Many things recurred to his mind of which he had not thought for years: and many others, which he had always considered innocent, appeared then to be heinous sins in the sight of God. The more he thought, the more rapidly his sins rushed into his mind; and he began to repent of his undertaking, and to shrink from the unwelcome vision; but then found that it was impossible to prevent his sins from rushing into view. His sins were set in order before his eyes and the sight, he thought was more than he could bear. He began to see clearly that, on the ground of good works, he was gone; for his evil deeds exceeded his good ones: and like a drowning man, catching at every straw, and almost in a state of desperation, he suddenly turned his mind to the other side, to see if he could not find more good deeds, that he might yet if possible, have enough to balance his sins. But upon the first sight of his good works, he saw to his utter astonishment, to use his own language, that they were all good for nothing. His confusion was great! He knew not what to do. The foundation upon which

K 2

he had stood for more than half a century, was swept away, and he was left in a state of despair. His sins appeared like mountains before him, ready to crush him into hell, and he had nothing to set a ainst them. He thought then that none could be so great a sinner as he. Instead of having done much for God, to promote his glory, as he had vainly imagined, he had done nothing at all. His whole life had been but one continual act of sin and rebellion against God; and he saw no way by which it was possible for him to escape eternal woe. He thought he must be damned and that justly.

Mr. Cushman visited him. and found him almost in the borders of complete despair. He talked constantly, and often mentioned his abused priviliges, lamenting his past life. in which he had done nothing for God, and bemoaned his fate. Mr. C. spoke to him upon the efficacy of Christ's death, the fulness of the atonement for sinners, and the Omnipotency of the Spirit; he replied, that it was too late; there was no mercy

for him; his happiness was for ever at an
end. They went to conference that evening. and he took an early opportunity to
address the assembly. He then talked as
he never did before. In a very feeling
manner, he warned the people, especially
the youths, of their iminent danger while
impenitent, and solemnly admonished them,
not to put off the all important concerns of
eternity. For his obstinate blindness,
when he had been so often warned of his
danger, his utter neglect of God. awful ingratitude and wickednes. he was utterly
ruined : his misery had already begun, and
he then felt the torments of despair en-
kindled in his breast. His address made
a solemn impression upon the minds of the
people, which was not soon forgotten. In
this dispairing state he continued for some
days, lamenting, as he thought, his most
aggravated sin, his awful ingratitude to his
heavenly benefactor.

At length God appeared for his relief,
opened his eyes to see his Saviour, whose
righteousness was sufficient to cover all his

sins; and opened his heart to receive him as his all-sufficient Redeemer. A flood of divine light appeared to break in upon his soul, and fill him with joy inexpressible. A view. of the Saviour, dispelled those clouds of darkness which had so long hovered over his mind, and drove away his despair. Sorrow was immediately turned into joy, *beauty was given him for ashes, the oil of joy for mourning, and the garment of praise for the spirit of heaviness.* His translation out of darkness and despair into God's marvellous light, was so sudden and unexpected, that he could not forbear crying out, though alone, *glory to God!* He took the first opportunity to relate in publick, what the Lord had done for his soul. The relation was striking and interesting. In this conversion, the favour of God has been so evidently manifested, that the enemies of Christ, and his doctrine have been confounded. He has ever since sustained a character that is truly indicative of his renovation. He seems to be astonished beyond measure, that he should live so long

blind to the beauties of God's character,
and the excellency of religion.

Another remarkable instance of God's
abounding grace was exhibited in the conversion of a man of about thirty five, who
had lived in that town about three years,
without attending publick worship more
than two or three half days. When the
awakening began he made light of it, and
called it enthusiasm. His wife's sister
who then resided with him was one of the
first who was awakened out of the village;
and for some time, was the only one in that
neighbourhood who attended the conferences. Always when she returned from
those meetings, he was very inquisitive to
know what they were doing in the village:
what new instances of awakening; who
talked in meeting; what they said, &c.;
and turned it off with a degree of ridicule.
Not long after she went home to her father's
in Salem (N. Y.) and tarried a few weeks.
She obtained hope in Christ the morning
she went away, but did not make it known
till she returned. At evening, when the

time for the people to attend conference arrived, he felt the same anxiety to know what was going on in the village, as he expressed it; and knew of no one in the neighbourhood who was going, of whom he could inquire. He waited some time, and finally concluded that he must go himself. He had then never attended conference meeting in his life. When he entered the house, beheld the multitude of people which were collected, and saw for himself what was going on, he was astonished, and ready to exclaim *that the half had not been told him.* He was immediately struck with a sense of the reality and importance of religion; and was no longer disposed to treat the subject with ridicule or levity. He returned with a heavy heart, wounded conscience, and a solemn countenance. The next day was the Sabbath, and he attended meeting all day. Those sermons were the first he ever really heard, in all his life. He attended conference again in the evening, and prayer meeting on Monday morning. But at this meeting, something being

said which seemed to displease him; it
was suggested to him at once, that there
was nothing in religion, and he instantly
determined that he would have nothing to
do with it. He then resolved to drive away
his serious impressions, and get rid of his
concern of mind as soon as possible. Accordingly he went from the meeting to the
town, found some of his companions, and
agreed with them to go the next day a
hunting. The day arrived and he went in
pursuit of his game. He found however,
that he took himself with him, and that
his conscience could not be quieted. He
went the next day, still resolving to divert
his mind, and drive away his conviction;
but succeeded no better than before. It
not being convenient to go again the next
day, he turned his attention to some other
employment. But he found, before night,
that it was a vain thing to fight against
God any longer. Instead of driving away
the Spirit, and stifling his conviction, he
found that his anxiety for his soul, and
conviction of sin, constantly increased. To

silence the upbraidings of a guilty conscience, was absolutely impossible. Though his days were spent in diversion, and apparent cheerfulness, his nights were sleepless, and distressing beyond expression. He yielded, gave up the idea of banishing his fears in this manner, and of stiffling his conviction, and resolved once more to attend to the concerns of his soul in earnest. He again attended conference meetings; and when Mr. Cushman had a private conversation with him for the first time, he had kept all his feelings, resolutions and motives entirely to himsef. And even then he did not express what he really felt in his soul; but requested Mr. C. to call on him the next day. Mr. C. went to visit him, and when he had asked him how he felt. He said, he felt as though he were in a new world. He observed, that on returning from evening conference he was so borne down with a sense of his sins and guilt. that he durst not go to bed, for he thought if he went to sleep, he should certainly awake in hell. His family all retired, ignorant of his situation, and he sat up till it was very late. His conviction and distress increased, till he began to despair of escaping that wrath which he justly deserved.—There could be no mercy for him; and it was of little consequence how soon he knew the worst of his case. He tried to pray, but could say nothing. He concluded at length to go to bed, and risk the consequences. And as he reclined his head upon his pillow, in awful agony, he felt to give himself into the hands of God, to do with him as he pleased. If he must perish, as he thought was certain, and which he saw to be perfectly just, he would perish at the feet of Jesus. He fell immediately asleep, having had no rest before for about a week, and awoke in a new world. It was a new morning to him.— *Old things were passed away, and behold all things had become new:*—Every thing on which he gazed appeared to be full of God—and all nature seemed to unite with him in praising the Redeemer; such love as he then had for the character of God

L

exceeded any thing, of which before he
had any idea. He thought he loved his
family before; but never did he have that
affection for them which then seemed to
flow from his heart. And the people of
God appeared to him exceedingly precious; whereas before, he almost despised
them. When he came to examine the
scriptures upon the distinguishing system
of God's grace, and of his minutely and
extensively, ordering and governing every
part of the Universe, he found his heart in
perfect unison with them. Who can deny
the special grace of God, when they behold such a trophy as this?

I will mention another very striking instance of conquering grace. This subject
is a British soldier, who served under Lord
Wellington in Spain, Portugal and France.
At the conclusion of the war in Europe,
he was sent to Canada; and was in the
battle of Plattsburgh. He then deserted
and came into Vermont. He came into
Fair-Haven sometime previous to the
awakening, and lived in a family about two

miles from the village. When he first heard about this work he was so profoundly ignorant of any such thing, that he thought it was some great feast; but durst not expose his ignorance so much as to inquire. As the attention increased, the family where he lived began to attend the conferences, and he went with them. His mind was soon arrested. He laid aside his profanity and excessive drinking, to which he had long been addicted. and gave his mind wholly to the things of religion. As he attended to the subject his anxiety increased. But while he was in a measure convinced of sin, of his entire depravity, lost state by nature, and the certainty of eternal misery without repentance, his heart for a long time retained its hardness. He at length became discouraged, and formed the resolution in his mind, to give it all up. and have nothing more to do with the things of eternity. He went immediately to the tavern, with some of his old comrades, and drank, he said, more than he had before for some months. In this way,

he was determined to drown, if possible,
all serious impressions and thoughts. By
this time the minds of the family were very
deeply impressed. The man's wife was the
only professor before. Soon after, a doctor, who was a subject of the work, and
some others, were at the house, conversing
upon the things of religion ; and they sent
out to have him come in, that he might receive some of the benefit of the conversation. But he refused, having resolved to
avoid every thing that was calculated to
bring the subject of religion into mind.
When they were about to separate, they
proposed to have a prayer ; and sent out
again to have him attend : but he still refused. The doctor, in returning home,
went near where he was at work ; called
and conversed with him ; and urged it upon him to attend to the concerns of his soul.
At first he entirely refused to give any
heed to what was said to him. But as the
doctor persevered in setting forth to him
the importance of believing in God with
all his heart ; he finally concluded that he

would attend to the subject, and made a promise to the doctor to this effect. He did not forget his promise. In a day or two after, he was threshing in the barn, and being desirous of company, a neighbour agreed to come and thresh with him in the afternoon, provided it continued to storm so that he could not work out. The time arrived when he expected him; but the wind blew up from the west and seemed to promise fair weather. He was at once angry, and said, before he thought, *Damn the wind*. At which expression, though always accustomed to such language, he was immediately shocked in such a manner, that he almost fell to the floor. He sat down and was not able to stand for some time. He said, he never received such a violent shock before in all his life. The thunders of war, the fall of thousands at his side, the shrieks of the wounded, the groans of the dying, and prospect of instant death in the field of battle, never struck him with half the horrour. From that he began to see clearly the plague of

L 2

his own heart, and his awful rebellion
against the King of heaven. He made no
more attempts to drive away his concern;
but earnestly inquired *What he must do to
be saved.*

In a short time after, at a conference
meeting in the neighbourhood, as he sat
listening to the conversation, and musing
upon his situation, bemoaning his fate, considering himself lost and undone for ever,
on account of his sins : all on a sudden,
light seemed to break in upon his mind,
and love to God and men expanded his
heart. He was so full of unspeakable delight, that he could scarcely contain himself; he felt that he must then arise, proclaim the goodness and mercy of God, and
call upon the assembly to praise him : but
thought it would not do for such an ignorant, wicked creature as he, to say a word
before such an assembly. He found, however, that he could not suppress his feelings, and avoid breaking out in expressions
of praise to God, if he tarried there, he
arose and left the house. He went away

by himself, and gave full vent to his feelings, pouring out his soul before God. The
next conference meeting was on Lord's
day evening in the meeting house. He
attended, and could no longer refrain from
declaring, what God had done for his soul,
and giving his testimony to the excellency
of that religion which had filled his heart
with love to God and men. His tongue
was loosed to speak with the eloquence of
an orator. And while his soul seemed to
flow forth in raptures of love, joy, and
praise ; he expressed that deep humility,
repentance for sin, and sense of unworthi-
ness, that was strikingly convincing to all,
that it was the Spirit of God, that opened
his mouth. and gave him utterance. With
no relation that had been given in publick,
were the people of God more surprisingly
animated, and the wicked more sensibly
struck with amazement. To see him, who
but a short time before, was a profane
drunkard, thoughtless of God and fearless
of man ; who was extremely ignorant, and
never accustomed to speak before an as-

sembly, rise and display such eloquence in the cause of God, was enough to convince the boldest infidel of the truth of religion. It appeared that none could hear, and not acknowledge the mighty power of God.

God has wrought wonders in that town, whereof we are glad, and have reason to praise his name for ever. There, many instruments were used to accomplish his purposes concerning Zion. There, a surprising change has been wrought, even upon the face of the whole town : the young and the old, the rich and the poor, the learned and the unlettered, meet as brethren of one great family, and sweetly agree, *to follow on to know the Lord, and run the race that is set before them in the gospel, looking unto Jesus the author and finisher of their faith.* There, the church, once almost blotted out from under heaven, and their minister about to flee away, and seek a people who would hear and believe the gospel ; now abounds with converts of the first abilities, wealth, learning, and influence, that, that town can boast.   About

one hundred have joined that church.—
Some have united with the Methodists,
some with the Episcopalians, and some with
the Baptist.

God has delivered his cause from reproach, and laid waste the systems of infidels. These are confounded, and stand
with silent astonishment, to see such a
striking alteration, as evidently appears
in many old hardened sinners, who they
thought, were inaccessible to the influences
of religion. But they are not more astonished than many of the converts are themselves, to find such a change in their own
feelings, views, motives and desires.

Who can behold the blessed effects of
the religion of Jesus, and not be convinced
of its divine original? The men of the
world, however depraved, may see, that
the power of this religion upon the heart
breaks up confirmed habits of vice, sub-
dues the unruly passions, tames the fero-
cious temper, changes all the affections,
and makes the carnal man entirely a new
creature. *Therefore, if any man be in*

*Christ, he is a new creature: old things
are passed away; behold, all things are become new.*   Who is able to do this, but the
eternal God himself? Hence it is added.
*And all things are of God, who hath recon-
ciled us to himself by Jesus Christ.*

———

POULTNEY, (Vt.)

This and many other towns, were received about the same time on the West
side of the Green Mountain. In 1816 an
uncommon gloom spread over that whole
state. The season was truly alarming, and
every month through that year was whitened with frost or snow. This severe judgment seemed to produce a solemnity upon
the minds of multitudes; yet nothing appeared to promise a revival in Poultney
until September. In that month, a work
of grace began in one corner of the town.
The pious were held in a state of suspense,
between hope and fear, whether, it would
continue and spread its blessings, or take

its flight, and leave the people in their sins.

About this time, there was a singular occurrence in the centre of the town, which led some to believe, that the Spirit was mercifully hovering over its inhabitants. One evening towards twilight, a number of girls from eleven to fourteen years old, were merrily at play, on the broad steps of the Baptist Meetiug house, and were suddenly struck with solemn awe, without any visible cause, and retired sighing, and sobbing to an house, where they spent the evening in reading the bible and other good books. One, of these children, was the daughter of the Rev. C. Kendrick. Some of these, obtained a good hope through grace and have professed their Lord before men.

In October the work spread into different parts of the town. Meetings were crowded and many began to inquire, *What they should do to be saved.* This work was rapid; yet in a great degree, free from enthusiasm. About two hundred have been

hopefully brought to know Jesus, and rejoice in the riches of his salvation. One
hundred of this number have joined the
Baptist church. Many of the converts are
in the bloom of youth.

MIDDLETOWN, (Vt.)

In November 1816 the work began in
this town. Conferences increased in number, and were much crowded. The work
has been principally among youths; and
even children have shared a part of those
gracious influences, that have inclined
them to forsake all their vanities, and seek
first the kingdom of heaven. They were
brought to discover their exceeding vileness and guiltiness before an holy God.
They were generally led to see the justice
of their everlasting condemnation; and
that they never did, and never could do
any thing to recommend themselves to the
divine favour of Jehovah : that if they were
ever saved, it must be altogether by grace.

The exhortations of young converts, and those newly awakened, beyond any other means, have been owned and blessed of God, for the conviction and conversion of sinners. About fifty have joined the Baptist church, a number the Congregational, and some the Methodist society.

Pawlet has received much rain from this cloud of mercy. Ira seemed to lie under the heaviest part of that shower, and almost every family in that town was awakened, and many believed; not because of the sayings of converted souls from other towns, who testified that Jesus told them all things that they had ever done; for they felt his power themselves, and knew indeed that *he was the Christ, the Saviour of the world.*

Clarendon and Wallingford were some alarmed, and a few fled for refuge and found peace, through the atoning blood of the Lamb, which taketh away the sin of the world. Upon Mountholly, God was seen in glorious majesty. There, many souls who had known his power for four or five

M

years and some for more than twenty, were waiting to receive their Lord, and bid him a cordial welcome to their hearts and families. When they heard that he was travelling in righteousness, upon one part of that mountain, and appearing mighty to save; they left all, and went out, to behold the ensigns of his power, and to walk in the light of his countenance. About sixty were added to the Baptist church, of which the Rev. Mr. Packer is pastor.

DORSET.

In this town God has made his mighty power known, and more than fifty have joined the Congregational church, and a considerable number the Baptist.

Manchester has been visited, and many souls have been turned from the power of sin, to love holiness and keep the commandments of the Lord. The work has been glorious in the eyes of the righteous, and great numbers, from the best information obtained, have experienced the abounding grace of our Lord Jesus Christ.

It spread its renovating influences into Arlington and a part of Shaftsbury. In Townsend, God has wrought wondrously. This region was inveloped in spiritual darkness : but it is now a region of light. The sun of righteousness has arisen with healing in his wings, and a lustre now covers the summit of their hills. Little children under ten years of age, have been made to cry, hosanna to king Jesus ! It has been customary for these children to spend their intermissions at school as a prayer meeting. They appear as faithful as any Christians. One of them, asked her father to pray for her : he told her that he could not. She then asked him, if she might pray ? He gave her leave, and she kneeled down in the presence of her parents, and poured forth her fervent desires before him, who has said, *Suffer little children to come unto me and forbid them not, for of such is the kingdom of heaven.* That was an affecting scene, and will undoubtedly be remembered, by that family for many years. Her father's heart seemed to melt within him, and has since been hopefully converted.

Some of the most respectable men in that place have been heard to inquire in earnest, *What shall we do to be saved?* A number of them have been made the trophies of distinguishing grace. In one family, five have been brought to leave the ranks of the enemy, and unite with the people of God. Some others, who had denied the very existence of the Deity, are now dwelling upon the delightful theme, of Christ and him crucified.

Windhall, Peru and Jamaica have also been visited, and many who have long sat in the region and shadow of death have seen great light.

Cavendish and Ludlow with some other towns in their vicinity lying on the East side of the mountain, have been highly favoured a few years past with great grace, and many souls were turned unto the Lord.

We turn our attention again to view a

range of towns on the West side of the mountain, where thousands have been raised from this valley of dry bones, and the breath of inspiration has filled an exceeding great army with heavenly energy.

Rutland and Pittsford, though slow to believe, have not been entirely neglected. Prayer meetings were often held, and many saints strove for the unity of the spirit, and plead earnestly for Jesus to come among them, and manifest his glorious power for the salvation of souls. They often heard the noise of abundance of rain, and were frequently raised high in expectation, that God would appear in his glory to build up Zion among them ; but did not partake so extensively of his mercies as their neighbouring towns.

Castleton was moved almost universally to seek the Lord while he might be found, and to call upon him while he was near. The wicked were enabled by the spirit of the living God, to forsake their ways, and the unrighteous their thoughts, and to turn unto the Lord who had mercy upon them,

and unto our God, who did abundantly
pardon.

The glory of the Lord shown upon Ben-
son and Hubbarton.   More than two hundred were quickened, and with repentant
hearts received the gospel of Christ. Their
meetings were large, solemn, and seemed
to be near the gates of heaven.   Many
came boldly to the throne of Jesus, *to obtain mercy and find grace to help in time
of need.*

Brandon trembled at the exhibitions of
God's awful judgments that touched her
mountains, and spread desolation through
her fruitful vales.   Indications of a famine
alarmed many.   In October 1816 an unusual earnestness in prayer was manifested
among the members of the churches in that
town. Conference meetings were appointed, and people of every denomination attended.   It was not long before a number
of youths appeared to be under deep conviction.—In a few weeks, some were hopefully the subjects of a saving change.—
They began to speak in these meetings,

and the work became general among all
classes, in each society. In some of these
meetings the powerful energies, of the
Spirit were most remarkably felt.

The Rev. Mr. Hebard proposed to the
people to hold a concert of prayer at his
house on Lord's day morning, to commence before sun rise. This was concord-
ant to the views of many, who wished to
rise early on that day so distinguished of
God, and held sacred by all who love to
seek him, as their Almighty friend, and
Saviour. About forty met at his house
one morning, before the sun had poured
his beams upon their paths. On the first
Lord's day in Jan. 1817, at an early hour
a multitude assembled at his meeting house,
to call upon the Lord and to *worsship him
in the beauty of holiness.* A remarkable
stillness and solemnity were peculiar indications of the great concern, that the
whole congregation had upon their minds,
and the fixedness of their intentions to
know if possible, how they could escape
the wrath to come. Twenty nine were

received into the church and sat down at
the Lord's table to commemorate his death.
That day will not be forgotten. The re-
cords of eternity will disclose the views,
the sorrows, the comforts and the transporting satisfaction in which that people
participated. To them it seemed to be a
Pentecostal season.

Since the work began, more than one
hundred have joined that church; and
some who were made acquainted with the
love of Jesus have not joined any church;
but in other respects exhibit their constant
attachment to truth, and are steady at-
tendants upon publick worship. About
sixty have united with the Baptist church,
and a number with the Methodist society.
The Congregationalist and Baptist held
the monthly concert of prayer together.

Lo! what an entertaining sight
   Those friendly brethren prove,
Whose cheerful hearts in bands unite
   Of harmony and love!

SALISBURY.

The revivals that were so prevalent in this state in 1816, called up the attention of the people in the above town. God was pleased to use the Rev. B. Perkins as an instrument, in alarming many who had lived as though they never were to stand before the judgment seat of Christ, and calling others to remember the loving kindness and tender mercies of the Saviour, which they had once experienced.

The first time he preached in Salisbury, a young man was awakened, who had been an active servant of the enemy of all good. He lead in all the vain amusements of youth and gloried in transgression. Another man of about forty, who was a professed Universalist, was stripped of his delusive hopes, and trembled in expectation of finally sinking into the regions of blackness, and darkness for ever. In a conference meeting not long after, he arose and observed; I rise up before you, my friends and neighbours, as a monument, to warn you not to do as I have done. I am the greatest sinner on God's earth. The fabrick that I had built, foundation and all, are gone to atoms. I am such a great sinner, that I cannot be forgiven. There is no mercy for me! I dare not ask for mercy! I dare not ask any one to pray for me. I warn every one not to trust to that which I find, fails me, and which has ruined me. I can see how others may pass the *Red Sea,* and sing the song of deliverance—but there is no hope for me. While making these observations, keen anguish was depicted in his countenance, and tears streamed from his eyes. All seemed to feel the weight of what he said. Some wept for joy, and others appeared distressed on account of the danger to which they saw themselves exposed.

In a short time the young man obtained peace, and told the assembly what the Lord had done for his soul. At this meeting a number more was awakened. Among these, was a physician of good abilities, so smitten, that he trembled, and his strength left him to such a degree, that he could

not get into his own house, though but a
few steps, without being helped. His soul
was made free in about three days. On
one Lord's day evening about thirty persons arose and requested the prayers of
God's people, that their souls might be delivered from sin, and mercy reach their
troubled minds.

Many in that little village have tasted
and seen that the Lord is good. As they
have received Christ Jesus, may they all
be found walking in his ordinances, and
finally enter into that kingdom which cannot be moved.

Hancock may be mentioned as one of
the places through which the Saviour must
needs pass. Some backsliders have returned home to their Father's house, and
some have been brought by a way they
knew not, and have been led into the
pleasant paths of wisdom, where they enjoy beyond expression, the light of God's
countenance, and in his righteousness, are
they exalted all the day long.

As the Rev. Mr. Perkins, who had fre-

quently preached in that town, was passing
through it, in the time of the awakening;
a middle aged woman came out of her
house, called him by name, wringing her
hands, with her eyes swimming in tears
she exclaimed, Pray Sir, do! pray do tell
me what I shall do to be saved? I am ready
to die with distress: Pray tell me what I
shall do? It was so sudden, and the scene
so affecting, that he was unable for some
time to utter a sentence. However, he
gave her a full answer from scripture. *Believe in the Lord Jesus Christ and thou
shalt be saved;* adding at the same time,
that the veracity of God stands pledged
for its fulfilment. She replied, I cannot,
I do not know how to believe? do tell me
how to believe. I am such a sinner I do
not see how I can be forgiven. He told
her that all mankind were by nature in her
condition, and must have been for ever
lost without a Saviour. He declared unto
her the way of salvation through the atoning blood of Jesus; the necessity of repenting immediately, and laying hold up-

on eternal life. He prayed, and left her sobbing and trembling under the weight of condemnation. His heart seemed to flow out in prayer, and he could with feeling propriety have uttered the language of the poet, when he said,

> Show pity, Lord ; O Lord forgive ;
> Let a repenting rebel live ;
> Are not thy mercies large and free ?
> May not a sinner trust in thee ?

SHOREHAM.

Previously to the commencement of a revival in this town, great darkness and stupidity seemed to attend almost every soul. Yet all were constrained to acknowledge, that God appeared upon the wings of the winds dressed in awful vengeance, and frowned upon this guilty part of our country. The State fast was solemnly observed. Some members of the Baptist church were deeply impressed with the importance, of having another day of fast-

N

ing appointed, in which they should meet to beseech the Lord to revive his work among them, and extend the banners of his mercy over *a world lying in wickedness.*

Other societies appointed special meetings for humiliation and prayer. A few were so assisted, and obtained such liberty in pleading with God, that they were led to believe, that he would pour out his Spirit upon the people. Though he tarried for a season, yet they waited and felt assured that he would come.

This church sent a request to the Vermont Association, to appoint a particular day, and recommend it to be kept, by all the churches belonging to that body, as a day of fasting and prayer. This request met with a cordial reception, and the 15th of Oct. 1816 was appointed. The day broke, the shadows began to fly away, and nearly forty churches prostrated themselves before the throne, and besought God to glorify himself, in giving salvation to men. The Spirit descended, and almost every church in that Association, felt its powerful operations. More than seventy were made the happy subjects of grace in Shoreham, and about thirty five united with the above church. Eight hundred and sixty six were added to the churches of the Vermont Association in one year after the appointment of the above fast. Five hundred and ten to the Shaftsbury: One hundred and seventy eight to the Woodstock: Two hundred and nine to the Fairfield: Sixty five to the Barre, and one hundred and twenty four to the Danville Association. Thus we find, that one thousand, nine hundred, and fifty two, were added to the associated Baptist churches in Vermont in one year. Many churches received additions that belong to no association. The Congregational and Methodist churches received vast additions. It is highly probable, that more than six thousand souls were renewed in that state in the course of twelve months.

How must the heavens have rung with the joyful songs of angels, who gazed upon those thousands, coming by the mysterious influences of the Spirit, to their Lord; bowing willingly to his sceptre; and he condescending to make an everlasting covenant with them, *even the sure mercies of David! O the depth of the riches both of the wisdom and knowledge of God! how unsearchable are his judgments, and his ways past finding out!*

That heavenly calling, which the inhabitants of Vermont received will never be forgotten—the illustrations of vengeance and mercy that have been given there, the clear shining of justice, the amazing majesty of grace displayed in the redemption of souls, will be among the themes and the acclamations of eternity.

MIDDLEBURY.

The Spirit descended upon this town in 1816. Christians of every denomination arose from the dust, put on the garments of humility and appeared greatly engaged for the salvation of their fellow men. The work was very powerful, and multitudes were delivered *from the horrible pit and miry clay.* and placed upon the Rock of ages. The prayers of the pious President and instructors in the College in that town, came up before God, and twelve or fourteen of the students have been led willingly to learn of *Him*, who is meek and lowly in heart.

Cornwall. New-Haven. Vergennes, Ferrisbury, Addison and Charlotte. have been visited from on high, and large additions have been made to the churches of the different denominations. The work of the Lord still rises to our view in surveying Vermont. A revival began in Troy about the first of January 1818, and in April it was prevailing with surprising power.—Hundreds were under serious impressions, and daily crying, *What shall we do to be saved?* The neighbouring towns were becoming more attentive to the means of instruction, and more solicitous for the regular preaching of the gospel. Meetings were frequent and well attended. Those who had spent their days in ignorance and wickedness, were made to cry with solicitude, *God be merciful to us sinners.* Patten, Westfield, and Kelleysvale have been roused from spiritual slumber and begun to feel the vivifying rays of the sun of righteousness. The songs of Zion are heard in that wilderness.

———

GREENSBOROUGH.

In 1816 a few pious individuals desirous of training up their children in the nurture and admonition of the Lord, commenced a course of catechetical instruction on Lord's day mornings. This was done without any knowledge of a similar institution in the United States. Unwearied exertions were made to influence parents, in each district, to encourage their children to assemble for the purpose of reading the scriptures, and repeating the different catechisms. Within a few months schools were established in a number of towns in that vicinity, and the youths of every denomination united together in this interesting employment. In June 1817 there was an exhibition, at which one hundred and three children were examined in the scriptures, and in the different catechisms. That was a memorable season. The Spirit descended like a mighty rushing wind. Many of the dear youths, were at that time convicted of sin, and wept aloud. Parents were not long unaffected. Shortly after this very solemn exhibition, not only of what they had learned to recite, but of the influences of the Spirit, a number were seen rejoicing in the Lord.

A little girl, after her conversion entreated her mother, in the most tender and affectionate manner, *to flee from the wrath to come.* The exhortation produced the desired effect. The work continued during the summer. Whole families were converted. Thirty three who are parents have been subjects of this work. A child of twelve years of age came forward to join the church. Nine of the same family, who had been renewed since the exhibition in June, were joyful witnesses of this transaction. The whole number of conversions exceed one hundred.

From the Congregational Associations in Vermont much refreshing information has been obtained. From June 1816 to June 1817 six hundred had been added to the churches in Windham Association. In the town of Willington God has made an astonishing display of the power of his word. An awakening began on the first of December 1816 and within the short period of two months not less than two hundred were brought to sing the song of redeeming love.

In Pawlet and Rutland Associations, the Redeemer in his majesty has ridden prosperously, and his right hand has taught him terrible things. These Associations comprehend twenty six congregations. Of these twenty have been favoured with a season of refreshing from the presence of the Lord. The whole number, who have been hopefully brought into the kingdom

of God, considerably exceeds twelve hundred.

In Addison Association grace has abounded and the Redeemer's countenance has
given light, life and joy to many souls.
From the Royalton Association information has been received, that a revival commenced in Montpelier shortly after the
cession of the General Convention held in
that place. It is believed that one hundred and thirty have become the subjects
of this powerful work. Berlin, Williams-
town, Braintree, Randolph, Bethel and
Roxbury have been favoured with copious
effusions of the Holy Spirit. In Waitsfield
and Barre some very interesting symtoms
have appeared that they also will soon
come into the light, power and liberty of
the gospel. *Whom the Son maketh free, is
free indeed.*

In the Northwestern Association, the
Sun of righteousness has scattered his
healing beams on Burlington, Colchester,
Essex, Cambridge and Sheldon: and on
the town of Fairfax has shown with pe

culiar lustre.   Orange and Coos Associations, have had showers of grace; especially the towns of Danville. Barnet and
Peacham.   The Lord has verified his word
by perfecting praise from infant lips.

In passing over Vermont we find many
towns destitute of stated, regular preaching.   God has been mindful of them, and
has greatly blessed ministers of different
denominations in their endeavours to gather
souls from those ruff and obscure places
to Christ.   Among these we may present
Marshfield, Warren, Moretown, Duxbury,
Hancock and Fayston.   Upon these the
dew of heaven has descended, and the inhabitants of those mountainous regions
have been inclined to come unto the Lord
for salvation.   They came out with joy,
and were led forth with peace; the mountains and the hills seemed to break forth
before them into singing, and all the trees
of the fields clapped their hands.

Braintree and St. Johnsbury may be num-
bered among the towns that have been remarkably revived.   From these and many

other places I have received particular accounts, but find no event, or means by which the work commenced, that differs from other places already described, and therefore deem it not necessary to insert them.

The Lord has done great things for his people in that state. His goings have been seen in his sanctuaries. Proud infidels have been brought to bow to the sceptre of Immanuel. Stout hearted sinners who were far from righteousness have in many places, been made to fear and tremble before God; and many have been made monuments of his boundless mercy. He has filled the hearts of his children with joy, and their lips with praise. O may they be steadfast and unmoveable, always abounding in the work of the Lord, knowing that their labour is not in vain in the Lord.

Before I conclude my narrative of revivals in New-England, I must notice a few towns more that have seen the salvation of God, and heard the thunder of his power.

Colebrook was visited about the first of May 1815, by that Spirit who gives power to sinners to believe in Jesus. Some of the most giddy and thoughtless youths were arrested in their career of vanity. Their thoughts were turned upon the solemnities of death, judgment and eternity. Their eyes were opened to see their lost condition. Some were soon brought to an humble reliance on that Saviour *who came not to call the righteous but sinners to repentance.*

The work spread in every direction embracing sinners, of various denominations, of every age, and character, from children of seven, to men of eighty years. Three hundred at least have been made willing to be saved upon the plan of grace, in *this day of God's power.* These have joined the Baptist and Congregational churches, and other denominations in this or the adjacent towns. The most aged inhabitants have never before witnessed such an extensive and powerful work in this part of the land. God seemed to bless almost every one who spoke in his name; but one young man especially, who was a member of Williams' College: He came forward early in the work and professed Jesus before the world, and was approbated by the Baptist church of which the Rev. Mr. Babcock was pastor.

The Lord appeared in the administration of the ordinances of his church, and crowned with success the faithful dispensation of his gospel. The Spirit descended like showers of rain on many towns in that region.

In Winchester, Norfolk, New Marlborough, Sandisfield, Goshen, Cornwall and Salisbury, sinners hastened to Christ as clouds, and as doves fly to their windows. From the most correct information received, I conclude that seven hundred were born again in these towns, in the course of this revival.

Canton and Northington. In these towns a revival began under the preaching of Mr. P. Brockett who had just entered the ministry.

O

He commenced his labours in June 1817. His discourses were directed to the hearts of his hearers, and he soon saw tokens evincing that the time had come for God to display his power in the salvation of some souls in those assemblies. One evening after closing the usual exercises, five or six persons appearing distressed for their souls, he began to converse with them, upon the importance of their believing in Christ immediately. In a few moments about twenty drew near, exhibiting signs of woe that all was lost. Sighing and weeping became general among those who tarried in the school-house where the meeting was held. Those who were out of the door, began to crowd into the house. The Spirit came like a mighty rushing wind, and every soul seemed amazed, and felt some of its powerful energies. Some time was spent in exhortations and prayers. He appointed a meeting for the next morning, and notwithstanding the day was stormy, some came three miles. Other meetings were appointed and the work spread.

Mr. Brockett visited Canton, and Jesus soon began to make his power known in that town. Crowds flocked to hear the young preacher, and a general solemnity clothed every countenance. The work was rapid. In about two weeks fifty appeared to labour under deep impressions. No school-house could receive the multitudes who were disposed to hear the unsearchable riches of grace proclaimed. They were under the necessity of leaving the school-house and repairing to a fine grove which seemed to add weight to the solemn scene. It was a little pine eminence. To many, this was the mount of God. Here they saw his glory and felt the enraptured influences of his love. To this seemingly sacred spot, the people came and held their meetings through the summer. The work was principally among the youths. An awful sense, of their exposedness to divine vengeance, covered their faces with gloominess for some days, and filled their souls with inexpressible agony. Some were greatly concerned for

a few weeks; then they have been sweetly
melted into evangelical contrition for sin,
and made willing to surrender themselves
unreservedly to Christ.

About sixty have been brought into the
liberty of the gospel, of which they had
lived in ignorance.   Now they admire the
plan of grace and can say with the poet,

> Why were we made to hear his voice,
>   And enter while there's room,
> When thousands make a wretched choice,
>   And rather starve than come?

Since 1815, New-London, Waterford,
Graton, Columbia and Hamden have seen
tokens of the presence of God our Saviour.
In these towns the Spirit has spread its
benign influences.   Large accessions have
been made to the churches.

Before I close my accounts of New-
England, I would assure my readers, that
Christ has, in an eminent degree, displayed his distinguishing love, and his heavenly influences have fallen upon many towns
in Massachusetts.   These are, Colerain,

Oxford, Ward, Athol, Becket, Worcester, Shrewsbury, Framingham, Monson, Lecister, Oakham, Princeton, Hinsdale, Greenfield, Rayalston, Northbrookfield, Richmond, Hardwick, Belchertown, Lansborough, Ashburnham, Bridgewater, Easton, Sharon, Foxborough, Beverly, West-Brookfield, Charlestown, and Boston. The three Baptist churches in Boston have had additions made unto them daily of such as shall be saved. The Congregational church in Charlestown has received about seventy six in one year, and the Baptist church about twenty. In W. Brookfield a work has just commenced, and from the best information that I have obtained, it appears that hundreds are awakened, and many begin to speak, as with new tongues *the wonderful works of God.*

In Belchertown God has often been seen in glorious majesty, and his enemies have been turned from their wickedness, and now talk of his power, and admire the amiableness of his character, and the unsullied perfections of his government. A

most powerful work has recently begun
and progresses rapidly.   Fifty have joined
the Congregational church in one day, and
one hundred and fifty more were expected
to come forward as candidates in a few
weeks. The account before me, states that
about five hundred in the town are more
or less affected with the work.

It is believed that more than four thousand persons, within the towns just specified, have experienced grace, since the
commencement of 1815.

The towns in New-Hampshire from
which I have received accounts, that the
Lord has been among them, and is still
carrying on his work in some of them ; are
Exeter, Sandbornton, Mount Vernon,
Raymond, Hollis, New-Ipswick, Mason,
Nelson, New-Boston, New-Chester, Dan-
bnry, Pembroke, Canterbury, Henniker,
Claremont, Newport, and Loudon.   In
these towns about one thousand, at least,
have felt the all powerful agency of the
Holy Spirit, and have arisen from dead
works to praise the Lord our God.

From these five states only, what an host arises to our view! All clad in the spotless righteousness of Christ and moving onwards towards the heavens. In this great army are men, women and children, who once were darkness, but now light in the Lord. These are all new creatures, unless they have believed in vain. If they have been regenerated, they are no longer *under condemnation ; for the scriptures declare, that they have been made clean, pure, and holy ; to have a new heart, a right spirit ; to be renewed ; to be born again ; to be born of God ; to be made alive from the dead ; created in Christ Jesus unto good works.*

Reader, permit me to beseech you, to meditate upon these things, and duly examine your own heart. Try your views and exercises by the scriptures and be not deceived. Remember if you have known the sanctifying influences of the Spirit, you will love God supremely : you will love his word, his people, his ordinances, and your fellow men. You will choose to pray, watch over your words and actions, and deny yourself. You will turn from sin and every false way. If you have never known these things; how can you rest indifferent, and remain stupid when so many are crying unto God for mercy? A little beyond your sight, lies an immensity of misery, into which you must certainly sink, if you die in your sins. O now, escape for your life and come unto Jesus, who will in no wise cast away any who come unto him for salvation.

> Eternal wisdom has prepar'd
> A soul reviving feast,
> And bids your longing appetites
> The rich provision taste.

GREENWICH, (N. Y.)

Towards the close of 1815, a good work began in this town. Saints began to arise from a long and very stupid state of spiritual slumber, and to come into the light, and liberty of the sons of God. A few came forward and joined the church. This seemed to freshen the souls of many, and especially the conversion and exhortations of a young woman, who was greatly engaged in religion. With an humility truly amiable, and with an holy solemnity she conversed with many concerning their soul's eternal happiness. She seemed to seek every convenient opportunity, to recommend her Lord, and to plead with her young friends to seek him.

In the commencement of 1816 conference meetings were multiplied, and the church arose, leaving the things that were behind, having taken up the stumbling blocks, that she had lain in the way of sinners, and moved onward *towards the mark, for the prize of the high calling of God in Christ Jesus.* Four or five converts appeared on the Lord's side, told their experiences, and followed Jesus in his appointed way, and joined the church, about the 20th January. At the close of this month, the work spread into different parts of the town.

No particular providential events occurred as the visible means by which the work was either begun, or aided in its progress. The Spirit came in a very gentle manner, yet it powerfully convinced of sin, righteousness, and judgment. The preaching of the word; the solemn and fervent exhortations of young converts, and the administration of ordinances were all owned of the Lord and crowned with success.

In 1816, two hundred and fifty four joined the Baptist church of which the Rev. E. Barber is pastor. Twelve have been added since.

Notwithstanding, the work was powerful and rapid. and all ages from twelve to sixty years old, were gathered from the broad way that leads to hell and brought to Christ and his church, yet but little noise or confusion has been heard. through the whole transaction. Truly, the Lord wrought *according to the counsel of his will; that they should be to the praise of his glory.* A part of Easton and Jackson shared in these heavenly influences.

KINGSBURY.

This is a small town about three miles square; yet that merciful Saviour who knows every atom in the universe, has condescended to make that spot of earth like Bethel, where Jacob saw a way to heaven, and heard the voice of the Almighty, announcing promises to his trembling soul.

A small Baptist church was formed in this town, about twenty five years since, and have maintained their visibility, though often very low, and much discouraged.

There were a few who sighed, being grieved at the abounding of iniquity. These agreed to commence a prayer meeting on the first Monday evening in January 1816. A number of youths had previously agreed to meet in the same neighbourhood to join in vain amusement. But a number, notwithstanding, attended the prayer meeting: for it was a novelty in that place. The saints engaged in prayer, and the Highest heard and granted their petitions while they were presenting them before him. Many, of those who attended their party of pleasure, began to be serious even before the usual hour arrived for their separa- tion. They began to consider that Chris- tians were assembled in the same neigh- bourhood and carrying their case before the throne of heaven; while they were sporting along the brink of ruin. These thoughts brought anxiety upon their souls, and this was their last evening of hilarity.

Conference meetings were appointed and well attended. An unusual solemnity characterized those meetings. The Spirit seemed to overshadow the place, yet none came forward as having known Jesus, until June. Then three professed Christ, to the great joy of his church. The revi- val spread like the electrick fluid, into every part of the town. In July eighteen blooming youths. and one man of middle age came forward and owned Christ before the world. The work prevailed through that year, and some mercy drops have de- scended until 1818. Two hundred and twelve have been added to this church,

making about five hundred since its con-
stitution. None have joined the church
under ten years of age, though some give
evidence of a work of grace upon their
hearts who are only eight. The Lord has
brought some to know the riches of his
grace, of every condition, and character in
that region.

Moreau and Fort Edward have also heard
the word of the Lord, and many have left
their sins, and now are considered no longer
*strangers and foreigners, but fellow-citi-
zens with the saints, and of the household
of God, and are built upon the foundation
of the apostles and prophets, Jesus Christ
being the chief corner stone.*

In these revivals, God has most conspicuously owned the administration of the
ordinances, the prayers and exhortations of
young converts. Many have been awakened in seeing the candidates advancing
to own their Lord, and obey his reasona-
ble commands. Some have come weeping
and overwhelmed with fears and sorrows,
and gone away believing and rejoicing in

P

Christ; others, in hearing the experiences
of their intimate relatives or acquaintan-
ces, have been brought to reflect upon that
day in which the righteous will be taken
away from the congregation of the wicked,
and seated at the right hand of the Judge
of all worlds, and thought themselves sen-
tenced to sink into remediless ruin. *Woe
unto the wicked for it shall be ill with him,*
has fastened upon their souls, and they
found no rest until Christ opened to their
view the amazing merits of his atonement.

God has gloriously extended his arm of
mercy, over Hartford, Queensbury, Fort
Ann, Granville, Salem, and Cambridge,
and about eight hundred have professed
the religion of Jesus.

TROY.

The winter before the reformation in this
city, an apparent seriousness was observa-
ble. By persons of fashion it was called
an unusually dull winter. Balls, parties

and scenes of hilarity were less frequent and more thinly attended than formerly.

The work commenced about the first of January 1816. An holy fervour appeared among the pious, which was increased by instances of convictions and conversions of sinners. Among these, there was one of a peculiar character.

It was a young woman in the morning of life, who had not reached the years of maturity. The death of her father, which had taken place some time before, had made a deep and lasting impression on her tender mind. It was sudden and unexpected; and he left behind him a disconsolate widow, with a numerous train of weeping and dependent children. In the midst of their sorrows, this child was comforted by a pious friend sitting at her side, with the consideration that God would be her father, if she would put her trust in him. The impression then made was abiding; and her mind was some time afterwards aroused to a sense of the guilt and folly of her past life. Her distress soon arose to such a height, in the view of her sins against her heavenly Father, that she was obliged to abandon her business, retire into her closet, and prostrate herself before him.

It was upon her knees in fervent prayer and supplication, acknowledging her transgressions, and imploring forgiveness, that the God of mercy manifested himself to her, as the hearer of prayer, and one who pardoneth iniquity, transgression, and sin: and she rose rejoicing in the salvation of God her Saviour, her father and friend. What encouragement is this for poor, overwhelmed, and distressed sinners to repair to the throne of divine grace, and cast themselves on the Saviour of sinners ?

She bowed a convicted and condemned sinner; and rose under a sweet sense of pardoning mercy; and soon became a transported saint ?

After this period, the influences of the blessed Spirit began to be more generally diffused; and soon were distilled like dew, *and as small rain upon the tender herb, and as showers upon the grass.* Among children and youths, the work of grace spread with the greatest rapidity. Numbers from eight years old and upward were deeply convinced of their guilt and ruin by nature; and cried out in distress, *What shall we do to be saved?* It was affecting to hear those little creatures speak of the vanity and folly of their lives—talk of the wonders of redeeming love—and singing *Hosanna to the Son of David, blessed is he that cometh in the name of the Lord.*

Their exhortations and prayers for their young companions were crowned with astonishing success. They appeared to be the favoured instruments in the hands of God, of awakening, convincing, and converting each other; and in their little assemblies, they would all be melted in tears, in telling what God had done for their souls.

The effusions of the divine Spirit now became general, and extended to all classes of citizens. The holy flame spread from house to house, and from heart to heart, until whole families felt its sacred influence. Husbands and wives, parents and children, masters and servants, all saw their lost state by nature, and the necessity of a change. Under the awful load of their guilt, they cast themselves at the foot of the cross, and begged and cried for mercy. And there, mercy reached them, and raised them up, to rejoice together in the salvation of the gospel. Their houses now became houses for God ; their sorrows were converted into joys ; and their tears into songs of praise.

By this time, almost every part of the city became more or less the theatre of illustrious displays of divine power and grace. Publick assemblies on the Lord's day were crowded: private meetings, which were now held every evening in the week, were solemn, and silent as the grave. The hearts of their ministers were fired.— The prayers of churches were fervent ; and the publick mind seemed awed down before the majesty of divine grace, which laid the proudest sinner low. Infidelity was abashed—stood astonished—and shut her mouth. Scarcely a whisper was heard against a work in which the divine hand was so manifest. It was the almighty Redeemer riding forth in the midst of them in the triumphant chariot of his gospel, conquering and to conquer.

As in all the works of God, and in all revivals of religion, there is a great variety; so there was here in the mode of divine operation. Convictions, generally, were pungent and short; and transitions from guilt and horrour, often sudden and rapturous. While some were aroused by the terrours of the law, others were allured by the grace of the gospel; while one was called with a still small voice, another trembled under the thunders of Jehovah.

Were it practicable, I could detail many encouraging and remarkable instances of conversion during the progress of the work. A few only can be now noticed.

One little girl of twelve years of age, whose mind became deeply affected with a sense of her sins at the commencement of it, and so continued for several weeks

without any relief. She uniformly returned from almost all the meetings, overwhelmed in tears, and seemed bordering
on despair. She saw her other little companions snatched as brands from the burning; and heard them admiring, with raptures of joy, the grace and glory of the
gospel. But she was left under hardness
of heart, and looked up in impenitency of
soul. At length, she lost sight of herself,
and was overwhelmed with the boundless
love of the Son of God, in dying for such
guilty creatures. Eventually this love ab-
sorbed her whole soul, melted her into
deep contrition for her sins, and brought
her at the feet of Jesus. Now, she exclaimed, I am happy in the love of the lovely
Saviour. He has taken away the load of
my weighty guilt, and brought me out of
darkness into marvellous light. My soul
rejoices in him; all things around me
praise him; the world is new.

Another instance, more remarkable still,
was a young woman of about fifteen, whose
distress for sin had been deep and affect-

ing for several weeks, without obtaining
any hope of pardoning mercy. At length,
her whole life appeared unveiled to her
view; and she seemed placed on the verge
of destruction, with the torments of the
damned spread before her, into which she
felt she was just plunging. With her sins
pressing her down, and the flaming gulf of
eternal misery before her, she cried aloud
for mercy, mercy, mercy, to her compas-
sionate Saviour, or she must perish for
ever. She cried until she lost the power of
utterance, and then sat supported, trembling for about one hour, speechless, over
the pit of destruction. At the close of this
awful scene, which struck horrour through
the whole family, she suddenly burst out
in raptures of joy and praise, that she had
obtained deliverance. She was perfectly
sensible, as she afterwards said, during the
suspension of her bodily powers, and knew
distinctly all that passed.

It was a sight of the Lord Jesus, she
said, the almighty Saviour of sinners, that
gave her instant relief. He was present

ed to her view in all his mediatorial glory, as able and willing to save to the uttermost; and her shuddering soul clasped him in the arms of faith, and he bore her away as a brand from the everlasting burning.

Her liberated tongue now broke out in unknown strains, and her transported soul seemed rather in heaven than on earth for several weeks.

The only remaining instance which I shall mention, was a venerable father rising eighty years of age. He had been remarkable for his integrity and uprightness through the whole course of his life; and probably stood as high for his morality as any citizen in this country. But when he saw by the illuminating influences of the holy Spirit, that he had neglected his God, however honest he had been towards men; when he saw that he had loved and served the creature more than his Creator; when the sins of his heart as well as his life were unveiled to his view; he was disrobed of all his righteousness, and sunk into anguish and despair. Oh, it was then his God whom he had dishonoured! his great, his gracious, his good God, who had fed and clothed him all his life long, whom he had insulted. It was his condescending, bleeding, dying Saviour, whom he had slighted. He was an old sinner, just on the verge of time, ready to launch into eternity; there was therefore no hope for him. Such was the language of his horrour and guilt, accompanied with groans of tormenting despair, which continued for several weeks. The sympathy and tears of his friends could not comfort him. The prayers of the ministers of religion and of the church, could not deliver him. The encouragements and promises of the gospel, were not for him. He had slighted the everlasting joys of heaven; and hell seemed yawning for his eternal fall. He was, reader, one of the most affecting monuments of distressing guilt; whose streaming eyes, and wringing hands, and groaning heart, would have stung thine inmost soul. A venerable and affectionate father, dear to a large and respectable family, and esteemed and beloved by all—tottering on the verge of time, and all before him a dreadful eternity! In this hour of sad extremity, when every heart ached, and united cries ascended to the throne of God for his interposing mercy, the God of mercy came down for his deliverance!

He plucked him as a brand from the burning—led him to the ark of safety, the Lord Jesus Christ—and enabled him to put his trust in him for salvation. Now his despairing grief was assuaged, his flowing tears were dry, and his sighs and groans were converted into praises. His trembling hands were raised to the heavens, and his faltering tongue shouted aloud for joy. And all joined in thanksgiving and praise to almighty God, for such wondrous love, such boundless grace, such astonishing mercy.

But he was too rich a treasure to be left long on earth. His grateful and overflowing soul soon matured for heaven. Having had an opportunity of publickly dedicating himself to God, and obeying the dying command of his redeeming **Lord**, whom he felt bound to serve, and holding communion with his people, he was laid, in the course of a few weeks, on a bed of illness. There he languished for about ten days, under excruciating distress, with all the composure of a child of God, and with brightening prospects for the realms of glory.

When his dissolution drew nigh, in the full possession of all the powers of his mind, he called his beloved wife and numerous train of children and grand children around him, and gave them his patriarchal benediction. Having bid them all an affectionate farewell, and commended them to his heavenly Father by fervent prayer and supplication, like the good old patriarch Jacob, he gathered himself up in the bed and expired, with the full prospect of a joyful transition to fairer and brighter worlds on high. Oh, *Let me die the death of the righteous, and let my last end be like his.*

Q

From these interesting private occur-
rences, which took place during the triumph of divine grace in that city, you will
permit me to lead you to two of the most
publick joyful scenes which were displayed. On the first Lord's day in April, the
Rev. Mr. Maclay of New-York assisted
the Rev. Mr. Wayland, in inducting forty
nine converts into one of the most glorious ordinances of the gospel dispensation.
Thousands gazed with astonishment upon
those happy souls, who testified by their
evangelical conduct, that, *To obey is better
than sacrifice.* On the first Lord's day in
May, the first communion of the Presbyterian church, after the revival commenced. The day was fine, and a large congregation, of perhaps fifteen hundred or
two thousand people, crowded the house.
The services were appropriate: the attention was profound; all was solemn. When
the morning exercises were closed, about
one hundred persons came out from the
congregation, approached the desk, and
arranged themselves in columns before it.

In these ranks of grace were found husbands and wives, parents and children,
masters and servants. All descriptions of
characters, high and low, rich and poor,
bond and free, here met together; all monuments of the same rich and sovereign
grace. From the lisping child of ten years
old, to the venerable patriarch of eighty
two, with a large proportion of the finest
youths, composed this rare assemblage of
ransomed souls.

Thus arranged, they made a publick profession of their faith, and solemnly entered
into covenant with the Lord their God—
to be his now, and his for ever. The whole
sat down together at the table of their glorious Lord, and commemorated his dying
love.

The whole church, consisting of between
three and four hundred members, followed
at different tables in succession until they
had all communed with their exalted Head.
They joined in the general joy of the wondrous triumphs of redeeming love, and
sealed their engagement to be the Lord's.

It was remarked by some who were present, that never before had they seen and felt so much of heaven on earth. All was serious and solemn. Nearly two thousand people gazing on the wonders of redeeming love; and almost one fourth of that number feasting at the table of mercy, admiring and adoring the condescending God who had rescued them by his precious blood from everlasting ruin.

Surely the Lord was in this place: for the divine glory seemed to awe down their spirits, and fill their souls. It was to them the house of God; it was the gate of heaven.

O give thanks unto the Lord, for he is good; for his mercy endureth for ever.

From that period, for many months the work of divine grace gradually progressed, and has had the most happy effect in meliorating the state of society; in abashing immorality and vice; in cementing the citizens together in the bonds of unity and love; and in combining their exertions in promoting the glorious kingdom of our exalted Lord.

A generation is growing up to serve him, who are the hope of the church and the world. They may be instrumental in transmitting this fair inheritance to future generations, when we are gone off the stage. It may reach to thousands unborn; and its final result can only be measured by the immensity of eternity.

This work brought many into the churches, in this city. Concerning their additions, and the revival that has just commenced, the writer hopes to be able to give some information before the completion of this book.

In Greenbush, the Dutch Reformed church under the ministry of Rev. Mr. Westervelt, has experienced a very refreshing shower of divine grace. In a factory not far from Troy numbers were called out of darkness into God's marvellous light.

MIDDLETOWN, (N. Y.)

In 1815 an awakening commenced in

Q 2

this town. In hearing the relations of experiences, it was found, that many had concealed exercises of this nature, sometime before they were disposed to let the same be known. This circumstance seemed to prepare the way for the visible part of the work to proceed with greater rapidity, than it might otherwise have done. In a few weeks the work spread through every part of Rev. A. Jackson's congregation. A few enemies to the Christian religion began to manifest their hatred to this revival; but it soon became so general, and so powerful, that even infidelity itself blushed, and soon ceased to show its opposition. A profound solemnity reigned in every part of the society, and in all their meetings. Prayer meetings were appointed, and were so crowded that the largest houses in the society were not sufficient to bold the people. It soon became no uncommon thing to see from three to five hundred people at those prayer meetings, the greater part of whom manifested a deep concern for salvation. A general prayer meeting was appointed and attended once a week in the meeting house. At those meetings, the neighbouring ministers were invited to attend : and for three months, they never failed of having from one to six or seven ministers at a time to assist in carrying on the exercises of religious worship ; all of whom about thirteen, acknowledged, that to be the wonderful power of God. At those meetings, they generally had from four to seven or eight hundred people. A deep heart rending sense of sin, and particularly the sinfulness of the heart, followed with an admiration of the abounding grace and mercy of God in Christ Jesus to the chief of sinners, were the leading features of the work.

At those weekly meetings they never failed having one sermon, and generally a number of ministerial addresses. The publick attention was so extensively excited, that frequently people came from ten, fifteen and some more than twenty miles to those meetings, eager to see the wonderful power of God in the conviction, and hopeful conversion of sinners. Many of those visitors, it is believed, returned home under serious impressions, which have terminated well to themselves and useful to others.

All ages, all classes, ranks, and degrees of people, shared in that glorious, and gracious work of salvation. The stout hearted—the stubborn oak yielded to that *Wind that bloweth where it listeth*, with as much pliability as the supple willow. More than three hundred in that town, have been considered hopefully converted. These have joined the Methodist, Baptist, and Presbyterian churches.

We long to see thy churches full,
    That all the chosen race
May with one voice, and heart, and soul,
    Sing thy redeeming grace.

———

FRANKLIN, (N. Y.)
A gracious influence descended upon this

town in August 1815. God made use of a young man as a great instrument in awakening many. He had been under deep concern of mind for some time: the anguish of his soul had been so great, that it had occasioned some indisposition of body. He was greatly opposed to the Saviour's terms of reconciliation to the divine govornment. But at length his will was subdued, his heart melted into repentance, and his soul wafted on the wings of faith and love: and so great was his joy, that some people thought he was a little beside himself, and that much religion made him mad. His soul was so filled with love to God and compassion for sinners, that he went from house to house exhorting his young companions *to flee from the wrath to come.* An impression was made upon the minds of those, with whom he conversed. There soon began a visible *shaking among the dry bones,* and numbers who were dead in sins have been made alive unto God. How powerful is the sword of the Spirit, though wielded by a human arm, when Jehovah nerves it with strength !

Roxbury has received a copious shower of divine blessings, and more than one hundred and sixty have obeyed the Lord Jesus, and gone on their way rejoicing.

Harpersfield has heard the joyful tidings of salvation, and many have been inclined to come to Jesus, who has *made an everlasting covenant with them, even the sure mercies of David.*

Masonville has bowed before the majesty of the King of kings. His arrows have been sharp in the heart of his enemies, and bold transgressors have cried out, *God be merciful to us miserable sinners.*

Meredith has felt his powerful arm, and multitudes have not only been wounded, but healed by grace, and made alive.

Over the Butternutts, he bent his bow and his arrows went abroad among the people. The voice of his thunder was in the heaven : sinners trembled, and hell spread wide her gates. God found a ransom and saved his people from going down into the bottomless pit.

Over Unadilla, the Lord seemed to rend the thick darkness and come forth. The hard hearts of sinners *flowed down at his presence.* A new church arose, being constituted in due form, and now travels in the footsteps of those who have gone this way before them to enter that rest, *which remaineth for the people of the Most High.*

New Lisbon hath known that the Lord reigneth, *and can save unto the uttermost all who come unto God by him.* Many bold offenders have found him to be *gracious, slow to anger, abundant in goodness, forgiving iniquity, and transgression and sin.*

Middlefield has been revived. Their meetings have been crowded with anxious souls, bowing under a sense of their exposedness to endless misery. The children of God have become earnest and glowed with an heavenly ardour before the throne of grace. Their prayers were heard in heaven; the Lord has come down to deliver the captives, and to open the prison to those who were bound. About forty have lately come out into the libery of the gospel, owned their Lord and now are seen walking with his people, in the ways of wisdom.

Hartwich has received of *Christ's fulness and grace for grace.* The work was very rapid and powerful, but remarkably solemn and free from enthusiasm. Many of the subjects of this work were from among the most unpromising materials, for the spiritual building. Some had been Universalists, others Deists. Their moral habits, like the majority of those who profess these principles, in every clime, had been loose and very irreligious. They seemed ready to bid defiance to the thunder of Jehovah's law, and were disposed to treat with scorn and derision, the tenderest expressions of a Saviour's love. They despised the sanctuary of God, set at naught the Lord's day, and made the religion of a bleeding Saviour, the subject of popular ridicule and contempt. Coldness and stupidity like a congealing frost stopped all the external movings of pious zealousness.

Only a few frequented the solemn assemblies of the godly. Some who had professed Christ, turned away and *gave heed to seducing spirits and doctrines of devils.*

When this melancholy gloom had thickened into an Egyptian night over that region, and some time had rolled away without the falling of a single ray of light to comfort them, they like the mariners with Paul, *cast out anchor and wished for the day.* At length the Sun of righteousness seemed to arise upon them with *healing in his wings,* and the voice of the prophet rung in their ears, *Arise, shine, for thy light is come, and the glory of the Lord is risen upon thee. The day spring from on high visited them,* and they beheld the glory of the God of Israel like the spreading of the morning sunbeams upon the mountains—beautiful, mild and cheering. More than one hundred have professed the name of Christ. The change is vast in that place.

> Lions and beasts of savage name.
> Put on the temper of the Lamb.

R

Colchester has received a gracious visitation. This has roused the godly from spiritual slumbers, and made them very active and happy in the kingdom of our Lord. About forty have been added to a small church in that town.

———

NORWICH, (N. Y.)

In 1814 a Baptist and a Congregational church were constituted in this village. Both these churches were very small, but apparently zealous for the cause of their Redeemer. The people around them were notorious for vice and almost every species of wickedness. They were profane. They did not manifest that reverence towards God which divine worship usually produces. If the Lord's day could be distinguished from other days, it was by being more devoted to the pursuit of vanity, and the practice of iniquity. The youths were conformed to the course of this world. Nothing was more foreign to their desire than to attend to things of a serious or religious nature. Vain company was their delight, and vain amusements the object of their unwearied pursuit. It seemed as if the inhabitants of that village were left to fill up the measure of their iniquities, and to go on from one degree of wickedness to another, till the patience of God should be wearied, and he destroy them in his holy displeasure.

But in the midst of wrath, God remembered mercy. Believers who had entered into covenant with each other, were faithful. They illustrated the excellency of the Christian religion in their lives and conversation. Their faith was strong, and their love fervent. They seemed to manifest a more than ordinary attachment to one another. Their happy society could not but attract the attention of the irreligious and profane, and convince the world that they had been with Jesus. These sent up their sincerely ardent prayers for the outpouring of the Spirit.

In 1816 a special work commenced.—

Preachers were faithful and warm in their prayers and awakening in their sermons. The duty of believers, the folly and ingratitude of those who sleep in time of harvest, were set forth in an impressive manner. All seemed to feel sensible that something must be done, but many did not know how to do it. Conference meetings were set up and numbers attended. The brethren wished to pray and exhort sinners to repent, but not being accustomed to this work, they had many fears, lest they should not discharge their duty in such a manner as to recommend religion to unbelievers. At one meeting there was an account read of the revival of religion in Lenox Massachusetts. The people inquired with great solicitude whether these things were so. The subject was new to them. They sought for information with eager curiosity. They were ignorant of what God had been doing in our land.— It appeared as if they had never once reflected that Except they were *born again, they could not enter into the kingdom of God.*

On the evening of New-Year's day a certain class of the youths attended a ball in the village, and there was a conference at the same time. These were appointments very different in their nature, and many of the youths had severe struggles in their minds in determining at which place they should attend. It was a critical period. They halted between two opinions. They hesitated whether to serve God or indulge themselves in that vain amusement that never profited any of the human race. On the one hand satan tempted; on the other, conscience remonstrated. On the one hand they were solicited by their evil propensities to go and enjoy the pleasures of mirth, and the recreations of the ball-room; On the other, they were impressed by the Spirit of God to turn from vanity, and prepare to meet their God. It was emphatically a sealing time. They were called upon to act decisively. Some who had made preparations and were resolved to go to the place of recreation, afterwards began to hesitate. One young man par-

ticularly, who had been uncommonly im-
petuous in the pursuit of vanity, was deeply convicted of his sin the very day of the
appointment. And even after they were
assembled, some were so much affected
and so greatly distressed on account of
their conduct, that they left the ball-room
and sought relief in tears. Thus there,
was a striking contrast between the different pursuits of the youths. The occasion excited publick attention to a very
considerable degree, and we have reason
to believe that the event was favourable to
their highest interest.

From this time the work became general.
It was deep, rapid and surpassed the power
of mortals. There was scarcely a thoughtless mind in the whole village. Business
was in a great measure suspended. Religious meetings were attended almost every
day in the week. Saints were vigilent
and active, their faith was strong. Their
zeal was not enthusiam, but it was ardent
zeal, and they felt as if they had much to
do. They seemed to possess in an emi-

nent degree that which may be denominated religious action, which will always be manifested more or less in seasons of revival. They were not discouraged by the unbelief and obstinacy of others. The power of God communicated energy to their entreaties. With trembling and affectionate concern they went to their ungodly friends, who were distinguished for profligacy and infidelity, and conversed with them about Jesus Christ, the Saviour of sinners.

This was an unnatural and unwelcome theme, but they were not ashamed to introduce it. Impenitent sinners were astonished and alarmed. Many of them had never witnessed such a scene before. They were seriously impressed with a sense of their wickedness. They saw that their whole lives were one continual departure from God, and that the mercy which could rescue them from ruin would be infinite. They did not esteem sin to be a slight evil, or a kind of infirmity which deserved the compassion of God. They frankly con-

fessed their guilt, and the deep depravity
of human nature.   They saw that they
were justly condemned by the divine law;
that they could not justify themselves by
their own merits; and that nothing but
the blood of Christ could open a way for
their salvation. *His blood cleanseth from
all sins.*

Although it may be said that the majority of those who are the subjects of this
work are youths, yet it was by no means
confined to them.   The moralist has been
brought to acknowledge the insufficiency
of mere morality.   There was one man
particularly, who was often refered to as a
standard.   It was a remark frequently
made by the impenitent, that if this man
became a Christian, religion was necessary
for them also.   But this man we hope became a Christian.   Two others also, who
had for a long time advocated the doctrine
of Universal salvation, renounced their
errour, and became the trophies of divine
grace.

The subjects of this work had a very

deep and overwhelming sense of their guilt. The penalty of the divine law was set home to their consciences with great power. They felt themselves to be under its condemnation, and they were miserable. Their distress was extreme. Nothing that was said to them could engage their attention or lessen the anguish of their minds. But at the same time they possessed their reasoning faculty entire. It was not a senseless melancholy, or obstinate despair. It was not infatuation. Their pain appeared to be the result of a genuine conviction of sin. They were disconsolate, for eternal misery lay before them. As soon as they felt the joys of pardoned sin, their darkness was dispelled : they were calm and unspeakably happy.

Upwards of sixty have been added to the Congregational church, and more than one hundred to the Baptist. In this village, which was once the strong hold of satan, the operations of the Spirit have been very conspicuously displayed. Zion has had new accessions of strength. Here has been a great and unexpected change. Each of these churches have built a very neat and commodious house for publick worship. To these places, they resort with willing minds, and call on God to aid them to honour his cause, to walk before him with humility, hear his word with obedient souls, and *glorify their Father who is in heaven.*

MALONE, (N. Y.)

Though the people in this town enjoyed the privilege of hearing the gospel preached statedly for a number of years; yet only a few knew its joyful sound by experience, until the summer of 1816. Then the Spirit, with overpowering influences, came upon sinners, and large numbers sought the Saviour with all their hearts. This work rent in pieces the subterfuges of infidels; enstamped solemnity upon the countenances of the scoffing; raised the worldling to higher riches than gold; arrested the voluptuary in his course of pleasure; turned youths from their empty and deluded fancies, and in some degree impressed the minds of all with the momentous reflection, that an Almighty Being exists and governs all worlds. It did more: divisions among neighbours were amicably settled, and the most friendly feelings produced. It suppressed profane swearing, Sabbath breaking, gambling, and their accompaning evils, which are so disgraceful to society, and offensive to God. In families where satan reigned for years, and the name of Jehovah was every day blasphemed, there now may be heard, prayers and anthems of praise. *This is the Lord's doings and marvellous in* the eyes of all who behold the effects of his unmerited grace.

GOSHEN, (N. Y.)

The cloud of mercy that had been seen in this region, began to move over the above town in 1815, and a few drops descended in August. Forty or fifty were refreshed, and commenced their labours for that bread, *which if any man eat, he shall live for ever.* In September there was a shower indeed. Two hundred at least were hopefully converted, and more than one hundred others engaged in anxious inquiry. It extended into four congregations. In one of them it became general and powerful, beyond any thing ever before known in that region.

EATON, (N. Y.)

God's *righteousness is like the great mountains, and his judgments are a great deep.* This was made known in Eaton.—Death swept away a number, and their survivers applied their hearts to wisdom. The Spirit of God came among them, and the inhabitants viewed themselves upon slippery places, and the regions of woe spreading beneath them. Every child of God

seemed to fly into the chambers of mercy
and to plead before the throne, *Spare us O
Lord one year longer.* He heard, and made
the hearts of sinners soften. In April 1815
the work became general. Conferences
were crowded and every heart seemed to
feel its own awful depravity. Jesus was
present, and his power removed the weight
of guilt from many souls. About one hundred professed the Saviour in a few months
after the work commenced.

Cazanovia has been a very distinguished
place for religious revivals. From its first
settlement, the Spirit seemed to choose to
hover over it and cause many to experience
its astonishingly glorious energies.

In the summer of 1815 there appeared
an unusual attention among the people.
Two women came forward and offered
themselves to the Baptist church under
the care of Rev. J. Peck. The evening
before one of them made an offering of
herself, she made her mind known to her
husband, and desired his consent. He
possessed too much politeness to forbid

S

her; but the enmity of his heart arose against it. That night his mind was much distressed. He was called away from home the next day upon business, and cherished the hope that she would not attend the meeting: but on returning home he found that she had been, and was accepted. He could conceal his feelings no longer, and therefore, observed that the union between them was dissolved, and his comfort in this world was gone. She endeavoured to show him his mistaken views upon the subject, but all in vain; an higher power was necessary. No sleep remained for his eyes, nor slumber for his eye-lids that night. Before morning, a spirit seemed to reason with him, and to urge him to believe, that it was possible that she was about to obey her Lord's commands, and if this should be true, he was wrong to oppose her: with that, the iniquity of his heart was laid open to his view, and so dreadful was the vision of that night, that he concluded, there was no peace for him in time or in eternity.

Nevertheless, he was not reconciled to

his wife, for he still thought her to be the cause of his trouble. In the morning his mind was full of anguish, and he thought if his wife were out of sight, his distress would abate, and he should obtain some relief; accordingly he assisted in getting her ready to attend meeting. She entreated him to accompany her, but he refused. She went to the sanctuary, in a calm, serene manner, not doubting but that God who had bowed her will was able to subdue his also. Her absence afforded no relief to his troubled soul. His distress greatly increased ; the wrath of God seemed to lie heavy on his mind. He visited his fields, but they appeared clothed in sackcloth. He returned to his house and walked his room agonizing under condemnation. At length, his wife returned from meeting, with some friends, who called to see him ; but he refused to be seen of them for awhile. But soon the scene changed ; for, he who turneth *the shadow of death into the morning, and giveth songs in the night,* appeared for his relief. His heart seemed to melt within him, he confessed to his wife and all present, his criminal opposition, and desired forgiveness of God, and every creature. He came forward and joined the same church. A number were arrested on that occasion, and the work spread into different parts of the town. Young men and maidens, old men and children were alarmed, changed and brought home to zion, with songs of joy.

This work has been like a gentle rain, or *the waters of Shiloh that* move *softly,* yet so mighty as to bear down opposition, and stop the mouths of gainsayers. The Deists and Universalists have renounced their pernicious sentiments, and embraced the humbling doctrine of the Lord Jesus. Backsliders have returned with broken hearts, being fully convinced that those, who *Observe lying vanities forsake their own mercy.* Saints have blessed God for the rich exhibitions of his boundless grace. More than two hundred have been added to the Baptist, and a number to the Presbyterian church.

Smithville has had a season of spiritual ingathering. The first tokens, of the blessed work were seen at a conference meeting in December 1816. The disciples of Jesus were earnest in prayer, and seemed unwilling to retire from the place, without a sealing manifestation of the countenance of the Lord. They poured out their hearts before him, and entreated that he would revive his work. The Spirit came down, and its flaming influences penetrated every heart, and spread its enlightening and renewing power from house to house. The people appeared regardless of the inclemency of the weather, the unpleasantness of the travelling or any other impediment. They were deeply concerned for their souls, and therefore, congregated in multitudes in whatever place, salvation was proclaimed for such miserable sinners. Whole households were arrested by the mighty power of God, and brought into the glorious liberty of the gospel. A young lady who taught a school in that place, was an obstinate opposer of this work. She sought out many inventions to pour her contempt upon those who called upon Christ to save them, from *going down into the pit where they cannot hope in God's truth.* About the close of February 1817, the special influences of the Spirit awakened her soul and about twenty of her pupils. The operations of the Spirit were so powerful in that school, that the greater part, of one day was devoted to prayer and praise. *The glory of the Lord shone around them,* and the children *cried hosanna to the Son of David: Blessed is he that cometh in the name of the Lord: Hosanna in the highest.*

These converts were faithful in exhorting each other daily. It was astonishing to hear them invite, and exhort their fellow children, and youths to flee from the wrath to come. From the age of nine to forty five, about one hundred are hopeful converts in this town.

HOMER.

This is a town, over which angels have

gazed with more than common eagerness.
to understand the vast depths of regenerating influences, and swell their songs in
commemorating the victories of Immanuel.
Within the rounds of a few years, they
have had occasion to rejoice over more
than seven hundred repenting sinners.
There satan has been trodden under the
feet of the saints. There infidelity has
gnashed his teeth in dying agony. There
the sweet and saving voice of grace has
been heard, and deluded, wretched sinners
have listened with evangelical attention,
and entered the gates of Zion with ineffa-
ble satisfaction. To them Jesus has been
precious. One revival has followed another,
leaving a little time for converts to examine themselves and become established
in the truth, before another came with
greater power, bringing to Christ and his
church a greater number of souls.

In 1815 and 1816 the greater displays of
grace were made, than in any other period.
The Presbyterian church under the ministry of Rev. E. Walker and the Baptist

under the ministry of Rev. A. Bennet have received large additions.

The work spread into Truxton, where considerable numbers joined the church under the ministry of Rev. T. Punington. In Locke, it has seemed more powerful, and greater numbers have bowed to the sceptre of our exalted Redeemer.

Guilford has lately been awakened, and the work increases and extends its heavenly dews into other towns.

Fabius has been brought from a very low vale of despondency and almost entire wretchedness to lift up her voice to God in the heavens, and now is enjoying the vivifying streams of grace. The commencement of this good day of prosperity was under the instrumentality of Rev. E. Blakesley. He made that people a visit some time in the spring of 1818, and the Spirit of the Lord seemed to attend all their interviews. He soon moved from Connecticut and became their pastor. The work has increased rapidly, and from the best information, I may venture to say that about one hundred have joined the church, and many are anxiously concerned for their souls.

HENDERSON.

In this town, the wonders of illustrious grace have shone conspicuously in the salvation of souls since the beginning of 1815. The Lord in his infinite goodness made the Rev. E. Osgood an honoured instrument to awaken many in this and other towns around it. He was so happy as to have three sons and one daughter made willing in this day of God's power, to own their Lord before men, and exhibit clear evidences that they had been made alive by the power of the Spirit. A large number were brought home to Christ in that revival. Another began in 1817 which surpassed the former. The words of truth fell like peals of thunder among the stupid and hardened sons and daughters of iniquity. Every sermon, prayer, exhortation,

and every thing they saw and heard seemed to augment their condemnation. The
awakened called upon their minister and
the friends of the Redeemer to pray for
them and point out unto them the way of
salvation. Their sorrows, fears and the
weight of guilt under which they laboured,
were unutterable. Blessed be God, they
were not left to perish in their sins. Jesus
interposed and gave them peace. Many
gladly received his gracious word ; obeyed
his all cheering voice ; told what the Lord
had done for their souls, followed him in
his ordinances; the church abounded in
the work, and increased in numbers daily.

In Ellisburgh, the Saviour was known
moving in the chariot of his gospel and
calling sinners to repentance. Here, in
1815 the word was quick and powerful.

Lorraine, Denmark, Rodman, Lowville,
Brownville, Watertown, Rutland, Champion, and Adams. In these towns, distinguishing grace has gained a triumph,
that surpasses in glory, all that statesmen,
heroes and kings have obtained by their

wisdom, power and valour since the world
began. A solemn and wonderful engagedness of mind seemed to be almost universal. All meetings for vain amusements
were laid wholly aside, and the people appeared far more engaged to attend religious meetings, than they ever did carnal
diversions. Religion was the whole topick
of conversation in all their social visits.
Large numbers would go from town to
town on some of their special meetings,
and all join in aiding others to meditate
upon the great truths of the gospel, *and
run with patience the race set before them
looking unto Jesus the author and finisher
of their faith.*

Champion abounded in the work of the
Lord. The first Lord's day in April, thirty
eight were received into the church of
which Rev. N. Dutton was minister. The
first Lord's day in July sixty six, and additions have been made until one hundred
and fifty were received into that Congregational church, and a number into the
Baptist church in that town. In all this

cluster of towns, including Henderson, we
may charitably believe, that since the commencement of 1815 more than one thousand souls have been born again. Small
churches have increased with men as a
flock; ministers have been greatly encouraged in their labours : old professors
have been brought to the gates of heaven,
and panted to see the signal given that
they might pass the guards upon the bat-
tlements of glory and enter into *the joys
of their Lord.*

Ovid was favoured with a marvellous
work of the Spirit, towards the close of
1814. The pious drew near to God, and
besought him to make known his rich grace
in the salvation of the people. They soon
were encouraged in coming unto him who
never turns a deaf ear to those who call
upon him in truth. Worldly conversation
was dropped, *and the things that make for
peace, and accompany salvation* became
their theme.

Many opposers rose up against the power and progress of this work. These were

Universalists, Deists, the self-sufficient moralists, and every hypocrite that could get an opportunity to show his opinion. He who from the beginning has laid his plan, to bring down the lofty looks of men and *destroy the works of the devil*, soon made those stout hearted sinners either bow with unreserved submission to his influences, or retire confounded from the exhibitions of his omnipotence. This work was so glorious, that it seemed as if the very clouds dropped down with righteousness, and the whole regions were filled with hosts of angels singing, *Bring the ransomed rebels home.*

In about ten months, two hundred and fifty joined the Baptist church in that town, and some the Presbyterian. *So mightily grew the word of God, and prevailed.*

Hector has received some tokens of the divine goodness, and a number of hopeful conversions have taken place.

Brookfield, Cincinnatus, De Ruyter, German, Green, Petersburgh, Oxford, Lenox, Lisle, Manlius, Madison, Augusta,

T

Pompey, Preston, Sangersfield and Tully, have all been graciously visited with an outpouring of the divine Spirit. Some have been more distinguishingly blessed than others, in receiving a greater copiousness of influences from heaven, and beholding a greater multitude of sinners flocking to Jesus, like clouds, and like doves to their windows.

WINFIELD.

Early in the year 1816, there appeared an unusual attention to meetings. Conferences were crowded, and the countenances of the people indicated that the things of eternity must be regarded, or they be for ever miserable. The Rev. Mr. Phileo, who was then preaching in that place, felt so deeply impressed with the importance of devoting his whole time in this work, that he gave up his school and laid aside every weight, and entered with all his heart and strength into labours for the salvation of the people.

He went from house to house and conversed with all whom he could, and exhorted them to repent and believe the gospel. The Lord rendered those interviews happy, and of infinite value to many persons. The influences of grace spread into every part of the town, and more than two hundred have given convincing proof, that they were brought to love Jesus with all their hearts. These have been added to the Baptist, Methodist and Congregational churches.

———

WESTMORELAND.

In 1818 a revival commenced in this town. A very singular circumstance occurred demonstrating that all are in God's hands, and that he can use them, for the prostration of every high, imaginary system of men; and for the rapid advancement of his kingdom in the world. A man who was a strong advocate for the doctrine of the final restoration of all men, urged professors to set up conferences, which had been neglected. This surprised them, that he should urge them to this important undertaking. They went forward —The Lord made them feel his life giving presence in those meetings: Sinners were awakened; saints were moved by an internal influence, to take hold on strength— to be diligent—watchful, and active in the performance of every duty. About forty were brought out of darkness, and enabled to profess the Lord before the world.

Verona has received *an unction from the Holy One*, and about sixty have united with the Congregational church and a number with the Baptist.

Vernon begins to feel alarmed and some have found Christ, and now can say, *One thing we know, that whereas we were blind, now we see.* To them, Christ is altogether lovely, *and the chief among ten thousand.*

In Ithaca, a special attention was discovered in 1816, in Rev. W. Wisner's congregation, and has continued in a greater or less degree to the present time. During the autumn of 1817, and the fore part of that winter, the work was more powerful than at any former period.

The work has not been accompanied with noise—it has been still and deep—it was evidently the Lord's work, and where he touched he generally broke the heart, and produced a repentance, *that needeth not to be repented of.*

About ninety have been received into the Presbyterian church and numbers have obtained hopes who have not yet joined.

In Auburn, an astonishing revival has been progressing in a manner that clearly evinces the superintendence of the divine Hand, and the irresistible power and efficacy of the convincing Spirit of God.

The learned, as well as the unlearned infidel, has been made to tremble, and acknowledge himself as a lost and ruined creature! On the first Lord's day in August 1817, one hundred and forty were received into the Presbyterian church in that village, and it was believed that one hundred more at least, had hope in God through Christ Jesus.

There was an unusual tenderness and concern on the minds of the people in that place, and in that region of country. Instances of conversions occurred every day, and many of them strikingly demonstrated, the sovereignty of divine grace. The enlightened heaven-daring sinner!—the votaries of amusement and carnality!—and many an aged father and mother were seen in tears and filled with grief, that they had so long despised the Saviour, and wasted so much of their precious time in sin and wretchedness.

Christians began to be roused from their slumbers, and became sensible of their barrenness—as if they had just discovered that the Christian's life must be a life of activity and usefulness in the cause of his Master: not satisfied with merely asking once a year, or when driven with affliction, but with every breath, *Lord what wilt thou have me to do.*

This glorious work spread into Mentz

where there had been four general revivals
within twenty years. None exceeded in
power and glory the present. In eight
months, one hundred and forty five were
added to the Baptist church under the
ministry of Rev. J. Jefferies.

In Palmyra, the triumphs of grace have
been displayed. One hundred and fifty
have been hopefully brought to love and
obey the Saviour's voice.

Precious revivals have abounded in Otis-
co, Romulus, Lyons, Wolcott, Victor, Li-
vonia, Genoa, Lansing, Cayuga, Dryden,
Skaneateles, Ludlowville, Aurelius. Mos-
cow, Camillus, Onondaga. Geneva, Gains-
ville, Bloomfield, Rochester. Buffalo, Ham-
burg, Eden, Willinch, Pomfret, Mendon,
Phelps, Gorham, Lima, Avon, Pittsford,
Penfield, Middlebury and many towns by
which these are connected.

Within these, many new churches have
been organized, houses for publick worship
erected, and large congregations gathered,
who now hear the way of salvation proclaimed with clearness and great power.

The eyes of the blind have been opened; the ears of the deaf have been unstopped; the lame man has leaped as an hart, and the tongue of the dumb has sung. In the wilderness waters have broke out, and streams in the desert.

BRISTOL, (N. Y.)

Previously to June 1817, there was an increasing attention, particularly among youths. In this month, their impressions were so deep, their views so clear, and their fears, of being for ever miserable, so great, that their concern could no longer be concealed. They needed no arguments to convince them, that they were entirely depraved—that they *must be born again*—that this change must be produced by the mighty power of God.—These points of gospel doctrine were fixed in their hearts, and no vague use of words could irradiate what the Spirit had taught their understandings.

In July, some made a publick profession of the efficacy of grace upon their hearts, and their attachment to the Saviour. This was a solemn time; more than a thousand people were present, and none appeared to be disposed to make light of the transactions of that day. Many received deeper impressions than ever, and the work spread more rapidly. More than sixty persons in a few months were added to the Baptist church in that town.

The greatest number, who have been the subjects of this work, is found among youths and children. These have conducted with great propriety, when they were under concern, and when brought into the liberty of the sons of God. They have seldom spoken, except when called upon to relate the exercises of their minds. This they have done very willingly, but in a low tone of voice. They have spoken with great clearness upon the odious nature and consequences of sin—of their helpless, ruined condition, without the supreme agency of the Spirit to regenerate their hearts.—

When speaking of its quickening powers
upon their souls—their countenances would
beam with joyfulness, while they ascribed
all the praise to God, for the richness of
his grace, through which they had obtained all their hopes of eternal blessedness.
Many Universalists, and those *who go
about to establish their own righteousness*,
have been brought to abandon their pre-
posterous systems, and to rejoice in that
grace which reigns through the righteousness *of Christ unto eternal salvation*.

BROADALBIN. (N. Y.)

The people in this town had been very
stupid for some time before the revival began among them. On the first Lord's day
in December 1816, the Baptist church commemorated the sufferings and death of our
Lord. Even on this most important occasion when every communicant should sit
down at the feet of Jesus, clothed in humility and rejoice in the unsearchable and

boundless compassion of Christ; many complained of hardness of heart, darkness of mind, and languid affections.

Notwithstanding, all this complication of distress that bowed down their souls through the exercises of the day, they believed it to be their day to attend a conference in the evening. They accordingly met; and Jesus who came among his troubled disciples at Jerusalem, on the evening of the first day of the week, came by his Spirit, and rendered that meeting heavenly. Some were wounded in heart, who in view of their lost condition wept most bitterly. The work soon began to exhibit signs of omnipotence. The people willingly flocked together almost every evening, to hear and if possibly to know, what the Lord was doing, and what would become of their souls. The attention of all classes, from nine to fifty years of age, was arrested, and many *have tasted that the Lord is good.*

From Dec. 1816 to May 1817, seventy eight joined the Baptist church, and other

228 RELIGIOUS

denominations shared largely in this season of refreshing from the presence of the Lord.

Owasco, (N. Y.)

A most wonderful work of grace commenced in this place in 1816. Seventeen persons were added to the church in January. This number was rather unexpected, and produced a more than ordinary excitement in old professors, who generally before this had lain in a state of spiritual torpor. In February, Rev. Mr. Len Eych pastor of the above church, visited and preached in that part of his congregation bordering on the Skaneateles Lake. Here the power of God came down, and about thirty mostly young persons were soon discovered to be under the most pungent conviction. He appointed another meeting for the next week, and then found a very large assembly who in the time of worship appeared to be in tears. After closing meeting, he conversed with many and found some, under the most awful apprehensions of their ruin and wretchedness, while others were rejoicing in the hope of the gospel. This induced him to propose to his consistory, the appointment of a meeting for the examination of such as felt the freedom of offering themselves for church membership. By this time the flame had extended to every part of the society, and almost every day new cases occurred: Conferences were unusually thronged; God's children were awake to their best interest; additional places for meeting were appointed and generally crowded. The consistory had two meetings for the examination of candidates, about the last of February and first of March. Sixty seven came before their first meeting, and thirty four before their last meeting. One hundred and one joined the church on the first Lord's day in March and sat down at their Lord's table to commemorate his death.

As several young persons from Sandbeach congregation were present, when these candidates were examined, these returned home deeply impressed. That society had remained in a state of spiritual stupor: but the news of the large accession to the church of Owasco, together with the impressions made on the minds of those before mentioned, operated like an electrical spark: the flame spread with a rapidity unequalled by any thing ever before seen in that region. In the course of a few days there was scarcely a family in the neighbourhood, where there were not some, more or less, under serious impressions: and in some families, all who were not church members were anxiously inquiring what they should do to be saved. Conference meetings were heled on every evening in the week, except Saturday evening.

The Rev. Ten Eych appointed one evening in a week for religious conversation. This he found peculiarly serviceable. It had a happy tendency to give freedom to many, who were before backward to open the state of their minds: and many received encouragement in hearing the state of others. In May seventy one were examined and admitted to the communion of Sandbeach church. The work still progressed in Owasco, and every sermon seemed to have a tendency either of comforting or awakening some present. In July one hundred and forty were examined and admitted to the communion. In one year there were admitted into those two churches, three hundred and fifty one.

Reader, let me beseech you, to rise upon the wings of imagination and waft yourself away to one of their communions, and behold more than two hundred dear youths approaching the Table of the Lord, with evident tokens of deep humility, and solemnity, highly appreciating the worth of their precious souls, and loving the Saviour with all their hearts. Could you remain unaffected, unconcerned for your souls? Could you say, again, *have me excused from* becoming a Christian? Would you turn away, and pass on in sinning against heaven? If you are a disciple of Jesus,

your soul is refreshed with these good
tidings. You do rejoice that Jesus reigns,
that his churches rise and flourish; that
his ministers have souls for their hire;
and that his kingdom will very soon *fill
the whole earth, and all nations call him
blessed.*

In this revival God's Spirit has operated
differently on the minds of sinners from
any thing seen in some other places. In
relation to three fourths of those, who have
been the subjects of hopeful conversion;
the time between their first alarm, and
their being set free in the liberty of God's
children, has not exceeded two weeks;—
and respecting some, not more than half
that time.

Two instances I may here mention worthy of notice; a man who had previously
spoken disrespectfully of the work, was
with difficulty persuaded by his wife to
attend conference, that was held in his
neighbourhood. During the singing of the
last psalm, he was awakened to a sense of
his deplorable condition. This was on

Thursday afternoon. On Friday morning, he was distressed beyond any language to describe. On Saturday morning he appeared to be the most happy person, on this side the perfect mansions of endless glory. He rejoiced in the government of God, and seemed fully to approve of God's plan of saving sinners through the meritorious righteousness of Jesus Christ.

Another man, of seventy years, whose days had been wholly occupied in accumulating wealth, was awakened to a sense of his danger by a sudden death in his family, and in the course of a few days, was made to rejoice in the glorious hope the gospel presents.

The whole work has been free from noise confusion and enthusiasm; nay, while distress and anguish of heart were seen depicted in their countenances, they strove to keep the same concealed from others, until constrained to apply to some pious friends to pray for them, or give them some spiritual instruction.

Three fourths, at least, of those who have

joined the above churches, are between
the age of nine, and twenty five years, and
perhaps an equal number of both sexes.
These have been lead to own their un-
worthiness, wretchedness and entire sinfulness in a state of nature: that salvation
is alone by free, sovereign, rich grace
abounding to sinners through the atonement. In about two hundred families,
which compose the Owasco congregation,
one hundred and eighty have more or less
praying persons; and there are several
instances where every branch of the family
give evident tokens of a change of heart.
Many of these young converts promise fair
to be peculiarly useful to the church of
Christ. They manifest sincere repentance, humility, a confident reliance on the
all sufficient merits of a risen Redeemer,
and a heart glowing with the warmest affection to his cause and interest in the
world.

The wonders, Lord, thy love has wrought,
Exceed our praise, surmount our thought;
Should I attempt the long detail,
My speech would faint, my numbers fail.

SAG-HARBOUR, (Long-Island.)

About the middle of October 1815, the Spirit was poured out from on high in plentiful effusions. Before this period, a season of awful declension prevailed. A death-like sleep seemed to have seized both saints and sinners. The church was clothed in sackcloth; she appeared forsaken and desolate.—Her state was melancholy:—few, very few came up to her solemn feasts;—her children were discouraged; like Israel in a strange land, they seemed to have sung out their song, hung their harps on the willows, and sat down to die. The scene was truly dark and foreboding, and became more and more so every day. —*O my leanness, my leanness*, was the cry of every true child of God. The wicked sat their mouths against the heavens; vice, with giant boldness, marched through the streets; Sabbath-breaking, profaneness, and intemperance, threatened to sweep away every vestige of religion: the scriptures mouldered on the shelf; the ordinances were barren, and the Spirit of prayer seemed to have taken its everlasting flight to heaven :—That place was indeed *a valley of dry bones.* Rev. Mr. Gardiner the minister in that place, seemed to ascend a neighbouring hill, and survey with anguish the whitening ruins that lay below; his heart sunk at the prospect; and he exclaimed, in the language of the prophet, *Can these dry bones live?* Scarcely was the exclamation ended, when, to his utter astonishment, the breath *from the four winds* came; the slain began to stir—the dead to live. The scene was changed : the people of God began to awake ; their hearts were comforted. The strong expectation that the Lord was about to appear in his glory and build up Zion, excited them to fervent supplications, to vigorous exertions.

Meetings for conference and prayer, were multiplied. Religious conversation was introduced : the attention of the whole congregation was soon aroused. The place of worship was crowded : the silence of the grave pervaded the assembly ; the seriousness of eternity set on every countenance. Every ear was open, every eye was fixed; while the truth of God appeared to sink deeply into every heart. The wicked were brought to a stand; the consciences of many were awakened. Fearfulness surprised the hypocrite; sinners in zion trembled. The anxious inquiry was made, *What shall I do to be saved?* The terrours of the law seized the hearts of many. The work of the Lord increased daily; *sinners were born of God.* The prison doors were thrown open, the chains knocked off; and numbers, delivered from the bondage of satan, were made to rejoice in the liberty of the gospel.

The work gradually progressed until about the middle of December, when the Lord seemed to rise in his might, and make bare his arm. His Spirit now like *a mighty rushing wind,* seemed to sweep all before it: the youths, the middle aged, and the man of years, fell prostrate at the foot of the cross! Often did the cry for mercy, and the song of praise, at the same moment vibrate on the ear. The footsteps of Im-

manuel were seen in every family, and his
power felt by almost every heart. The
people of God who had witnessed several
revivals, filled with astonishment, would
often say, that they had never beheld such
a day as this before. Whenever they met
there was a cordial shaking of hands and
a smile of joy; while every other feeling
of the soul seemed to be swallowed up in
mutual love. So transporting was the
scene, and so elevated were the joys of
some elder Christians, that they seemed
almost really to believe that the glorious
morn of the latter day had commenced.

In that season of divine power, when
Christ rode forth from conquering to conquer, one hundred and twenty persons, in
the course of two months, expressed their
hope of having passed from death unto life.
These were of all ages from twelve to eighty
years. This work was remarkably still
and solemn. The work of conviction continued in most cases from one to three
weeks, before the subjects received divine
light and comfort. The veil, of sin and

darkness which covered their hearts, was in many instances taken away in a moment, and the light of *the Sun of righteousness,* like a flood poured in upon the benighted mind ; while in other instances, *the day spring from on high* was but just seen to glimmer, and the night of the soul to be gradually chased away as the shadows of the morning. All expressed great astonishment at their former stupidity and danger. They were overwhelmed to think that God had not cut them down, as cumberers of the ground, and sent them to everlasting misery. The way of salvation by Christ, was viewed as the only door of hope for a perishing world. They were filled with great solicitude for the welfare of careless sinners, and frequently exhorted them to press into the kingdom of God. Little associations, for prayer, in different parts of the congregation were formed among the young converts. These meetings, while they excited those, who attended them to search the scriptures, had a happy influence in uniting them to each other, in cherishing that love which God had shed abroad in their hearts.

There did not appear any external opposition to the work of the Spirit. It carried such unequivocal marks of supernatural power, as to astonish the hearts and stop the mouths of all. The whole face of that congregation has been changed in a religious and moral point of view. Intemperance, profaneness, and Sabbath-breaking have greatly diminished. The tide of iniquity, which swelled high, has begun to roll back, and continues to ebb. Numbers, who have been long habituated to the most disgraceful vices, have entirely abandoned them, and become correct members of society.

Mr. Gardiner's faithful conversation among his people, was greatly blessed. After preaching one day, he took a man by the hand who was eighty years of age, and said unto him, My dear Sir, you are, I perceive, an old man, standing on the borders of eternity. According to the course of nature, death will soon overtake you. It is of the highest importance that you be prepared to receive the summons, whenever it may come. You cannot stay here long. Your glass is almost run : your head is clothed with grey hairs : your limbs tremble with age.—Have you made your peace with God ? Have you ever repented of sin, and believed on the Lord Jesus Christ ? He shook his head : the tear started from his eye, and stole down his withered face, while his whole countenance bespoke the agitation of his heart. He had no more peace, until about two weeks after this, he found it through faith in the Redeemer. He was brought in at the eleventh hour, and praised God for the riches of his distinguishing grace.

Another man about seventy, and another of sixty, nearly by the same means have been awakened, and it is hoped are now the living monuments of mercy, and walk in the light and have fellowship with the saints.

I add one more circumstance, believing that it may edify some of my readers, and

W

I pray Christ that it might awaken every
lady who may peruse it.

Mr. G. and Mr. S. in visiting the people,
called at Mr. E's. and found Mrs. E. under very deep conviction—prayed with
her—and after stating to her briefly the
way of salvation by Christ, and the importance of surrendering up her soul to him;
he urged her to this duty by various motives, and as he pressed the duty of immediately surrendering her soul and body,
and all she had into the hands of the Lord,
her distress increased every moment; until overwhelmed, she fell down upon her
knees and poured out her soul to God for
more than two hours. During her praying,
among other things she said, as far as they
could recollect, O, Lord, I am a great sinner; the worst sinner in the world, I have
sinned against great light for thirty years.
Gracious Father, I pray that thou wouldst
be pleased to pardon my sins, through the
blood of Jesus. I am growing worse every
moment: Lord take me as I am; I shall
never be any better. O Lord, take me

now, this moment; I shall never be more
willing, unless thou make me willing, to
give myself to Christ.   Hast thou not pro-
mised to receive the soul that submits to
thee? O Lord, why am I so unwilling to
give up? O blessed Jesus! if thou dost not
receive my soul now it will perish justly.
I know I deserve to be destroyed for ever:
let thy face shine, and dispel this night that
hangs on my poor soul.   Precious Saviour!
take possession of my heart; give me the
light of thy countenance: Lord Jesus, take
me as I am this moment; I am willing to
give up: I give all to thee: and O that
thou wouldst be all in all to my poor soul:
O may I believe: I do believe: O Lord I
can do more: O Jesus thou art precious;
make me a heart Christian; make me, Lord
Jesus, all that a Christian can be: I want
to be such a Christian, O Lord, if I am
any: I hope, O Lord, I have given up to
thee.   Search me and try me; search my
soul, as thou didst Jerusalem, with can-
dles: take from me every thing that is offensive to thee.   Shed abroad thy love now

in my heart; it is sweeter than honey. O give me words to praise thee; thou hast done a great work for me, as I humbly hope: I would give thee the glory. She paused for a moment and then said, If there is any idol left, O help me to give up to thee. Lord, I give up my husband, my child, my brother, my sisters into thy hands: do with them as seemeth good in thy sight. Bless all their souls: and may I and they live to God.

This lady has since professed religion.

East-Hampton that has been so often the theatre of divine wonders has been highly favoured. About one hundred have obtained hope, and a considerable number of them have joined the church.

———

SHELTER ISLAND, (L. I. Sound.)

This little spot of earth rising amid the flowing sea, and lifting itself above the highest wave, was a place to which the drunkards of other regions came, and unhallowed fishermen drew up their nets, and hailed their wicked companions, as having arrived to a shelter from Sinai's arrows and the multitudinous sounds of gospel trumpeters. There, a population, not exceeding three hundred, poured down their thirsty throats eleven hogsheads of rum annually. These profane violaters of the laws of God and man, *regarded not the work of the Lord, neither did they consider the operation of his hands,* that were declared to them, by those who had been eye witnesses of the goings of our God and King.

Amid these outrageous sinners, a few pious Christians were found, who resorted to a little sanctuary on Lord's days and poured out prayers to the Saviour of sinners to come and make known his great power. They did not call in vain, for they soon found Him there, *Whom the heaven of heavens cannot contain.* A revolution on that *little isle of the ocean,* was clearly effected, not by the might and power of man, but by the Spirit of the Lord of hosts, through the instrumentality of those, who abounded not in gifts of eloquence, but in the work of faith, in the labour of love, and the patience of hope.

The Lord has brought a number to love him, and a church of about sixty members assemble in unity, and walk as children of the day. The rum drinkers are so scarce, that one hogshead supplies their demands through the year.

We can easily learn, why the lovers of rum, and all other haters of Christ, ridicule revivals of religion, pure doctrinal preaching, and a revelation from heaven. For these all declare that *Our God will come and will not keep silence. A fire shall burn before him, and it shall be very tempestuous round about him. He shall call to the heavens above, and to the earth beneath that he may judge his people.* What a terrifick time!—when the heavens shall be shrivelled as a scroll, and the elements melt with fervent heat! When the earth and its appendages shall be burnt up and the fury of the conflagration be such, that *there shall be no more sea?* A time when the noble and ignoble dead, the small and the great shall stand before God, and be judged according to their works! Yea, a time, when the thoughts of the heart and every secret thing, shall be brought to light! When the innumerable millions of transgressions in embryo, and abortive sins shall be exhibited in all their purposes and intents! A time when justice, eternal justice—shall sit alone on the throne, and pronounce a sentence, as impartial, as irrevocable; and as awful as eternal! There is a term of human life; and every human being is rapidly gliding to it, as fast as the wings of time, in their onward motion incomprehensibly swift, can carry him! And shall not the living lay this to heart?—And shall we not live in order to die? Should we not die in order to be judged? And should we not live and die, so as to live again to all eternity; not with Satan and his angels, but with God and his saints? O thou man of God! thou Christian, thou immortal spirit, think of these things!

NEWARK, (N. J.)

There has not been many places on
earth, where the Lord has so often, and so
universally brought the people to experience the greatness of his grace as in that
village. The last revival began to make
its appearance in Dec. 1816 in their evening conferences. The Spirit seemed like
a gentle wind to fill almost imperceptibly
every part of the village at the same time.
The first day of 1817 will undoubtedly be
remembered by many, in that place in time,
and in eternity. There prevailed on that
day, as has since been made known, a
general impression of seriousness on the
minds of the people. They could not account for it; nor did they, as individuals,
know that others were exercised in the
same manner as themselves. It was, doubtless, an invisible influence, the effects of
which have since been abundantly manifested. On the first Monday evening, at
the concert of prayer, many attended and
some felt greatly distressed, and wept bitterly. From that time, there were meet-

ings in some part of the village every evening, and crowded with people. The ministers and leading members in the churches visited and received visits constantly every day for three months. In almost every house as soon as they entered, they heard the cries of the wounded, or expressions of joy from those who had been brought into the liberty of the gospel.

Numbers of the subjects of this work, are heads of families; but more youths have professed to be interested in that refreshing season than any other class. Some had been the most notoriously wicked of any in the town; others were of the most securely self-righteous among the Pharisees. It is truly delightful to contemplate the effects of divine grace on such a variety of characters.

In about ten months from its commencement, there have been hopefully brought into the knowledge of the truth, two hundred of the first Presbyterian society, one hundred and seventy of whom have been received into communion. Ninety seven

were added to the second church. **Sixty**
five to the Baptist church and a number to
the Methodist society.

In Elizabethtown, a revival, more general than any which that congregation has
ever before experienced, began to make its
appearance about the first of February
1817, and in a few months one hundred
and sixty persons were received into communion; and many others had obtained
hopes, and rejoiced greatly in the Lord
their Redeemer.

In Connecticut-Farms, the revival began about the same time, and a number
made a profession of their faith.

In Bloomfield and Patterson, the Lord
has appeared merciful and very gracious.

In Orange the work was very powerful.
In about three months from its commencement; three hundred persons had been
very deeply interested about the salvation
of their souls, and two hundred entertained a hope that they had passed from death
unto life.

Woodbridge, Rockaway, Perth-Amboy,

Jersey, Newfoundland, and North-Hardiston, have been specially blessed. In the second congregation of Woodbridge, the revival began in the autumn of 1817, and more than one hundred and twenty have been added to the church as the fruits of this gracious work.

The commencement of the revival in Rockaway was about the same time. In that congregation it is worthy of remark, that the first appearances of the special presence of the divine Spirit were manifest in a Sabbath-School. The number of subjects of this work, added to that church were one hundred and twenty.

In some of these towns, the faithful labours of missionaries, have been owned of God, and many persons brought under powerful convictions, and led to inquire what they should do to be saved.

In South-Hampton, Oysterponds, Sterling, Mattituck, and Huntington on Long-Island, it has pleased the Lord to revive the languishing graces of his people, and to awaken many of the careless to seek the salvation of their souls.

PRINCETON COLLEGE, (N. J).

For nearly a year before this gracious
work attracted publick attention, the students attended on all the religious exercises and instructions of the College with
more than ordinary seriousness; and the
minds of some of them as has since appeared, were ripening to be the first fruits
of that harvest of souls. This seriousness increased in the winter and spring of
1815, and many could no longer keep this
invisible. Every religious service, both
on secular days and on Lord's days, was
attended with a solemnity which was sensible and impressive. In this manner the
revival commenced, or rather became apparent, in the second week of January,
without any unusual occurrence in providence :—without any alarming event ;—
without any extraordinary preaching, without special instruction, or rather means
that might be supposed peculiarly adapted
to interest the mind. The divine influences seemed to descend like the silent
dew of heaven ; and in about four weeks,

there were very few individuals in the
College edifice who were not deeply impressed with a sense of the importance of
spiritual and eternal things. There was
scarcely a room—perhaps not one—which
was not a place of earnest secret devotion.
For a time it appeared as if every student
was pressing into the kingdom of God; so
that at length the inquiry, in regard to
them, was, not who was engaged about religion? but who was not? After this state
of things had continued, without much va-
riation, for about two months, it became
manifest that a change was taking place.
Some were becoming confirmed in the
hopes and habits of evangelical piety; some
were yet serious, thoughtful and prayerful,
though perhaps not in so great a degree,
or at least not so apparently, as once they
had been; while some were plainly losing
the impressions which they had lately felt.
The result was, that more than forty in
that time of refreshing gave favourable
evidences, that they had been made the
subjects of renewing grace. And nearly

X

the whole of the remainder showed a great readiness to attend on all the social exercises of religion ; not only on those which were stated and customary, but those which were occasional, and the attendance on which was entirely voluntary.

The special means used to promote and cherish that revival, besides the circumstances already mentioned, were the following.—A short address on the subject of religion was made, after prayers, on every Saturday evening. In preaching on the Lord's day morning, subjects were selected suited to the existing state of the College.—A particular reference was often made to the religious attention which had been excited among the students, in the remarks which accompanied their bible recitations. A weekly lecture, intended for the students exclusively, was given by the President, on Tuesday evening. A social prayer meeting was held, on every Friday evening, at which one of the Theological professors commonly made an address. A family prayer meeting, as the students called it, was, every evening held among themselves, at which a large proportion of the whole College attended. Smaller and more select associations for prayer were also formed. The individuals whose minds were anxious and labouring, were, as often as they requested it, carefully conversed and prayed with in private. Finally, writings of approved character, on doctrinal and practical religion, were pointed out and recommended to the perusal of the students; and a short system of questions and counsel was drawn up by the President, for the use of those who began to cherish the hope that they had entered on a life of practical piety.

There was no sectarian spirit accompanying or mingling with that revival. There were students in the College belonging to four or five different denominations of Christians. At first, there appeared to be some apprehension in the minds of those who were not Presbyterians, lest they should be drawn into a union with this denomination, if they yielded to the sentiments and feelings which began to be prevalent. But the President told them in his first address, on Friday evening, that it was his fixed purpose to inculcate no doctrine or tenet that was not found in all the publick orthodox creeds of protestant Christendom—that he was indeed earnestly desirous that they all should become real practical Christians, but that he had no wish to make a single proselyte. This had a tendency to remove every apprehension—and the intimation then given has been sacredly regarded. Every thing has been general. The great doctrines of the gospel have been exclusively inculcated. May Christ visit every College and fill those fountains of science with the riches of his immense grace.

Trenton and Bound Brook have been visited with times of refreshing from the divine presence. In Baskenridge the Spirit of the Lord has been poured out in copious effusions. The good work, which commenced in the Academy, was soon extended, and the churches of our Lord were replenished.   A goodly number of the students of that institution, as well as many others, have joined themselves to the Lord.

In Morristown, a work of grace commenced in August 1815 which had been slow and gradual in its progress, and deep and solemn in its effects.   The numbers of its subjects are very considerable.

In the city of Philadelphia, a very animating revival commenced in January 1815. A deep, silent, and awful work—attended by pungent convictions of sinfulness, and misery, continued for some length of time. The Spirit has not yet withdrawn from that city.   Many are still brought to love the Saviour and the churches are daily increasing with men as with a flock.

Blockley has lately been visited in mercy.   Numbers have been hopefully brought to know Christ and the power of his resurrection.   Forty have joined the Baptist church under the ministry of Rev. Mr. Ashton.

A revival has recently begun in New-Milford Penn. and in many other towns in

that state, of which, the writer, would most
cordially give the publick some more soul
edifying information, had he received correct accounts relative to the commencement of the work and its effects, upon
those congregations in which it has spread
its divine energies.

Since 1815, there has been a powerful
work of the Spirit in Montage N. J. About
one hundred and sixty have professed the
religion of Christ.   Also in Brookfield N.
J. more than one hundred and seventy have
professedly experienced grace, and united
with the people of God.

BALTIMORE.

In September 1817 Rev. Mr. Davis, a
Methodist preacher, who was stationed at
Fell's Point, proposed in one of his meetings, that all who would keep each Friday
as a day of fasting and prayer, should assemble in their meeting house, and spend
an hour or more in solemn worship.   A

number of the members at once came into
the measure, and sacredly regarded the
day as an occasion of dedicating themselves more fully to God. The happy effects of this were soon realized in those
who assembled together. They were in-
structed by their pastor in particular, to
pray for a revival of religion in their own
souls, in their families, classes, and congregations. With encouraging appearances among themselves, they went on in
this good work until about the commencement of the New Year, when it pleased
God to show them, that their prayers were
heard, and that they should not eat their
morsel alone; but that their neighbours
should be brought in to share with them
the rich repast, and taste the wonders of
redeeming love.

An inquiry began among the unrenewed,
what they should do to be saved: the keen-
est conviction seized their minds, and they
began to turn to the testimonies of the
Lord. This pleasing change in individuals
was only as the refreshing drops before a

plentiful and glorious shower. In a few
weeks the congregation became uncommonly numerous. Solemnity sat on almost
every countenance, and souls seemed to feel
more or less the mighty power of God.
Convictions were powerful, and many came
before the altar requesting prayers and
instructions from the devoutly engaged
servants of Christ, that they might obtain
salvation through his precious blood, even
the forgiveness of their sins. Here many
were enabled to give up themselves to
Christ, and obtain peace in believing, and
joy in the Holy Ghost. In the course of
six or seven weeks, five hundred whites,
and nearly one hundred coloured persons,
have in that charge, been added to the
church.

The work spread very rapidly, and their
prayer meetings were so crowded, that
they were obliged to open their meeting
houses to accommodate the multitudes who
came. Their meeting house on the Point
has been opened and generally filled almost every night, for five or six weeks;

and their meeting house in Old Town was opened almost every night, and hundreds attended.

In these meetings many were awakened, and some at almost every one of them, were converted. Their class-meetings surpassed any thing ever before known in that region. In some cases, after the leader had closed by prayer, the members continued for a considerable time on their knees, praying earnestly to God for a free and full pardon of all their sins. Like blind Bartimeus, *They cried a great deal for mercy:* and some *immediately received their sight and followed Jesus in the way,* shouting glory to God in the highest.

Private families have been visited, and some children and servants have been so overwhelmed with distress, that they have been heard in their secret retirements, to cry out for God, amid the dark watches of the night, to save their sinking souls; and to some the Sun of righteousness has arisen with healing in his beams, before the natural sun had appeared to usher in the day.

The abodes of human degradation and woe have been visited by an all gracious God. The heavenly fire has been kindled up in the Penitentiary. A number of the criminals professed to feel his divine influences and to believe in Jesus. Such was the displays of grace among the people, that in four weeks, between three and four hundred white people joined the Methodist church in town.

Many heads of families, of respectable standing, and a great number of young men and women of good families and promising in their appearances, were among the subjects of this work: and some sinners of the deepest die have witnessed that Christ could save the chief of sinners.

In some cases, the work of conviction has been progressive; in others very quick and powerful. Some have drunk the wormwood and the gall of repentance for weeks, before they have found peace: others have in a few hours found salvation in Jesus, and felt that their sins were forgiven. God works in his own way, and to him be all the glory.

A revival has appeared in Suffolk circuit, and a number of souls have been made the happy subjects of regeneration.

Haupogues was the first place that shared in the gracious visitation. Meetings were attended almost every evening, and convictions and conversions increased. Dwelling houses were not sufficiently capacious to contain the people who assembled to witness the marvellous displays of the power of God. They seemed to forget or pay but little attention to their ordinary concerns, while the more important business of eternity engrossed their thoughts. Under preaching, the word seemed to be as eagerly received as a morsel of meat by a hungry man.

Westfield was the next that was favoured with the effusions of the Spirit, though it was sometime in a doubtful case. The cloud seemed long to hover over them, till suddenly it poured forth its rich treasure; and the day so much desired opened with peculiar lustre. Some souls were converted in a prayer meeting, and many returned home under a consciousness of their guilt and absolute need of a Saviour. This was the beginning of good days. Frequently, after preaching the congregation would remain upon their seats, as if unwilling to leave the consecrated spot. Not only were sinners awakened and converted, but Christians were built up in the Lord, and backsliders reclaimed from their Laodicean security.

Soon after this, the work began in Patchogue; a place once notorious for inattention to religion, especially among the youths, who were much given to the vain recreations of life; and professors in general had become formal, and slept among the dead. But suddenly the place assumed a different appearance and the people in general became alarmed. The youths who were once so eager to pursue their vain delights, now saw their frivolity, and deeply bewailed their folly and miss-spent moments. Instead of the nightly revel and unprofitable conversation, companies met together to pray with, and for each other, and improve their time with reference to a future state. Conversions were numerous, and many of them clear and convincing. About one hundred souls, it was hopefully thought were made the subjects of pardoning grace.

In Moriches, Islip, Babylon, and Stonybrook was a similar work, and many were brought from darkness to light and from the power of Satan to God.

In these revivals were seen pious parents rejoicing over their sons and daughters, crying for mercy, or testifying of the goodness of God in their late conversion ;—or perhaps, children praying over weeping, broken hearted parents. Human language cannot express the solemn, the delightful, joyful sensations that pervade the hearts of the righteous on these occasions.

Southhold, Long-Island, has received the grace of God. The work commenced about the last of July 1818 under the preaching of a Baptist minister who visited that place, from Connecticut. His labours were principally confined to the upper

Y.

part of the town. It was not long before
the work found an easy transition into the
Methodist,   and   Presbyterian   societies.
This soon roused every friend of Christ to
action, and a very pleasing harvest of souls
were gathered into these churches, whose
hearts were, we hope, prepared by grace
to own the Saviour before the world, and
who will adorn his doctrine in their lives
and conversation.

President Edwards says, That it has
been God's usual manner in every new establishment of his visible church, to give
a remarkable outpouring of his Spirit. And
even we find that the Lord remembers his
people, who migrate for the important purpose, of being more useful in spreading
more extensively the banners of grace, and
preaching the gospel where Jesus had not
been named. Christ will come into every
place whither he has sent his servants.
Therefore, we hear of his reign in our Western regions. Ohio has not been left a
barren wilderness. There the Spirit has
awakened thousands, and converts are be-

coming very numerous. In Austinburg, Morgan, Rome, Jefferson, Lebanon, Ashtabula, Geneva, Harpersfield and Madison, the Lord has moved in majesty and appeared mighty to save. Great numbers of youths, and young married persons have been born again : yet in some instances those who have lived in sin and rebellion against God, forty, fifty or sixty years, and have been scoffers or neglecters of religion have been brought to bow to the sceptre of Immanuel.

In Athens, (the seat of the Ohio University,) God has entered and made himself known to many. Grace has abounded, Christ has been honoured, and sinners have seen his salvation. Since 1815, Ohio and Indiana have been increasingly anxious to enjoy the ministry of reconciliation, and in some of their borders, the servants of Jesus have entered, *not with carnal weapons*, but with those which have been *mighty through God to the pulling down of strong holds: Casting down imaginations, and every high thing that exalteth*

*itself against the knomledge of God, and
bringing into captivity every thought to
the obedience of Christ.*

It has been stated to the writer, by a
missionary of distinguished talents and
piety, who had ranged the state of Indiana,
that about one half of the heads of families
were esteemed truly religious, and prayed
daily to God for an outpouring of his Spirit.

Kentucky has been advancing towards
the mount of God.   The thunders of Sinai
have prostrated many of her lofty heroes in
infidelity.   They have been brought to confess that Jesus is the Christ, and has all
power in heaven and earth.   Powerful
awakenings have been spreading through
many of her towns ; new churches have
been formed, and old ones have received
great additions.

In many Presbyteries, the work has been
glorious.   But especially in Logan, Elk,
Nashville and W. Lexington.   At several
of their camp and sacramental meetings,
the heavens seemed to bow, and the glorious displays of divine power were ex-

tensively seen and felt. Many were pricked in their hearts, and heavy laden under a sense of their guilt, fell prostrate in the dust before a sin hating and sin avenging God, and were constrained to cry out, *What shall we do to be saved?* The compassion of the adorable Redeemer was exhibited to their view. Their darkened understandings were illumined by the powerful beams of the Sun of righteousness, and their hearts were subdued to the obedience of faith. They believed, adored, wept, and rejoiced, *with joy unspeakable and full of glory.* In about four months in 1817, one hundred in those meetings professed regeneration; the most of whom appeared very clear in their views of the glorious scheme of redemption.

In Concord, Mount Pleasant, and Paris, the work has been particularly conspicuous. There has also been considerable attention and solemnity in Fleming, Smyrna, Point Pleasant, Sugarridge, Springfield, and Augusta congregations; and many other places present prospects of a very encouraging nature. Y 2

To the Baptist churches in Elkhorn Association, five hundred were added in 1817,
to Long Run, six hundred, and to Franklin three hundred and fifty.

In Tennessee, the gospel has been attended with some pleasing manifestations
of heavenly influence. About four hundred were added to the Baptist associations
in 1817. From other denominations I have
not been so happy, as to obtain correct information of the doings of God with them.

In the Illinois and Missouri Territories,
extensive fields for missionary labours are
laid open, and Christ has shed a lustre upon those enterprising souls who have entered in his name to gather a people for
his praise and glory. Churches have been
formed as palaces in which he will dwell,
and from which, he will send out fresh
orders for the inhabitants of the wilderness to draw near and worship before him
in the beauty of holiness.

Mississippi and Louisana begin to hear
and tremble before the Lord. His Boaner-
ges have begun to attack the strong holds

of Satan; to penetrate the dark recesses of infidels; to march amid the thickening hosts of Indian tribes; to draw the sword of the Spirit, and with an humble boldness to demand in the name of the King of heaven, all men to *Repent and believe the gospel.* Conquest begins to hover over their banners and the number of the slain increases. Churches are formed and the ordinances of the gospel are administered, where the campaign was first opened.— Move on ye soldiers of Jesus, fearless of danger, of sufferings and of death. Never sheathe your swords until your feet are washed in the waves of the Pacific Ocean, and the songs of converts roll along those skies through which you shall pass, to be *crowned with an eternal weight of glory.*

St. Louis, begins to receive the good tidings of the gospel and live. A revival has begun, a church has been formed, and converts are multiplying.

Francisville has also been alarmed. A few nave become acquainted with the power of the gospel and owned a Saviour before their ignorant neighbours.

New-Orleans has been penetrated by zealous missionaries. Many assemble to hear what these men can tell them about Christ and him crucified. Some divine influences have been experienced.

Upon the Carolinas and Georgia some showers of grace have descended, and a considerable number of souls have sprung into life. Those who love Zion begin to put on their beautiful garments, *for the time to favour her, yea the set time is come.*

Several churches in Virginia have been richly visited with showers of divine goodness. Happy and extensive revivals have been witnessed. In Mecklenburg, Charlotte, Lunenburg, Sandy Creek, Meherrin, Norfolk, Petersburg, Winchester, Leesburg, Fredericksburg, and Richmond, the number of praying people is increasing, religious excitements have prevailed, and many have been added to the churches, of such whose names it is hoped are in the book of life.

In the District of Columbia, religious influence has been experienced; and especially in Georgetown and Alexandria. In these towns God has opened the fountain of his superabounding grace, and inclined a number of souls to receive of its fulness.

The writer would insert many particular accounts from the Southern regions, if it were practicable. Much interesting information has just arrived from different states, over which he has already been, and upon which he has dwelt with more than ordinary satisfaction. A few brief extracts must for the present suffice his readers.

New-York city. This London of America has received *an unction from the holy One.* The Spirit of the Lord has displayed its omnipotence, and brought multitudes into the kingdom of God our Saviour and built his churches *with lively stones.*

The greatest increase has been made to the Baptist church under the ministry of the Rev. J. Chase. In fourteen months two hundred and sixty have been added to that church. The last communication dated Dec. 1818, stated that the work was still spreading, and that, that people had resolved to build an house for publick worship, 65 by 85 feet; their present house not being large enough to receive the multitude who press to hear Mr. Chase. He was ordained their pastor on the 27th May 1817. His labours have been remarkably blessed. Many have also been awakened and comforted in beholding the ordinances administered.

Christians of different denominations in that city have become very active, and abound in good works. The Lord is multiplying their numbers, and giving them great light and divine influences.

Mount Pleasant received some divine manifestations of God's mercy, in 1817 and about forty professed the Lord Jesus before the world.

Catskill has felt the power of the word of reconciliation, and some have been brought to embrace the humbling doctrine of the cross.

In July 1818 there were some appearances in Cairo, that raised the expectations of many Christians that the Lord was about to change the hearts of multitudes. Children and youths were greatly awakened. How many have been converted, or how far the work has extended the writer has not been able to learn.

Hudson has seen a day of visitation.—About the commencement of 1817 sinners began to be awakened, and saints encouraged. Meetings were held almost every night in the week, and deep concern seemed to spread through the city. Rev. Mr. Stanton and Rev. A. Briggs were very much engaged to have their flocks, all press into the kingdom of Christ. Their labours have been abundantly blessed, and they have received about sixty into each of their churches. These have shown by well ordered lives and conversation, that they have not believed in vain. The Methodist society has received some.

In Schodack the work has been gradually progressing for nearly two years. Sixty have united with the Baptist church. Nassau has also been revived. Cambridge has not been the least among these towns; for unto many of them, Jesus has *become wisdom, righteousness and sanctification.*

In Orange, (formerly Cliftonpark) renovating grace has continued to abound to many, for nearly ten months. It is now spreading into many congregations.

Since 1815 Schenectady has been under some awakenings, and a considerable number have been converted. There are now some favourable appearances of another revival.

TROY.

In the 185 page, I gave my readers some encouragement to look for more information concerning God's former displays of grace in this city, and the present revival, and now have the satisfaction of laying before them, the following.

Since the commencement of 1815, there have been received into the communion of the Presbyterian church, two hundred and sixty—into the Baptist, two hundred and twenty five, and into the Methodist, three hundred and twenty—and a number into the Episcopalian communion. These were the fruits of those astonishing influences experienced in this small city.

The present revival commenced its visibility on the second Lord's day evening in January 1819, after the usual religious exercises were closed in the Methodist church. A few young people tarried to sing after the congregation was dismissed. A preacher who was raised up in this city being present on a visit, observed one of the number affected, and after some conversation with this young person, who requested him to pray, a number came to the altar, and the Spirit descended and spread its influences upon that people, until nearly two hundred have joined the church.

In relating their experiences, they profess to have been seriously impressed from different periods of time; none probably exceeding a year.

The danger of procrastination, and par-

Z

ticularly as it procures hardness of heart, has been faithfully proclaimed in their ears, and the Spirit has set the word home to their hearts. Almost the whole of that congregation exhibit signs of great seriousness.

The work is now increasing among all the denominations in the city. Upon the fourth of February, Rev. Mr. Sommer, observes that he had conversed with thirty five since the 26 of January, who have felt the powerful influences of grace. Some of them have been approved by the standing committee of the church, as suitable candidates for the ordinances.

The means, by which it has been the pleasure of Jehovah to originate and carry on the work among his people, have been as various as the application has been sovereign. Several of the converts, are scholars in the Sabbath School and some of them date their first impressions from the affectionate exhortations of their pious teachers; while others, make mention of the preaching of the everlasting gospel as the instrument of their conversion to God.

Rev. J. Coe D. D. observes that it seems almost too much to expect a general revival, in so short a time since the other. But that we ought not to limit a God of boundless mercy. He works like himself. Many little children, and some young people, and others further advanced in life, appear to be solemnly impressed. That very considerable divine influence is diffused among his congregation, in awakening, and convincing them of their guilt and danger. But where this will issue God only knows, and time must determine. They rejoice with trembling. Yet may they with an holy pleasure look up and utter the language of Isaiah, *Who are these that fly as a cloud, and as doves to their windows?*

ALBANY.

Since the commencement of 1815 a divine influence has been exerted in this city, and the gates of our Zion have been thronged with anxious sinners and joyful converts. But the cloud that hung over the city of Troy, fraught with divine compassion, passed around us, only letting here and there a few drops fall to refresh and cheer this thirsty hill of God.

In 1816, the truly pious of all denominations had their expectation greatly raised, and were daily expecting a copious shower of grace they could even hear the thunder of God's power and see some who had been careless seeking a refuge for their Christless souls ; yet he who governs the universe, *and will have mercy upon whom he will have mercy*, has not come down with such overwhelming influences, as upon some other cities.

His spirit seems to have been hovering over us, and though often grieved with our hardness of heart and maleconduct, yet being slow to anger and abundant in mercy, has not withdrawn from us, nor given us over to work out our eternal condemnation.

In the summer of 1816 a revival began in the Baptist society and about forty professed to cherish hopes in a Saviour's merits; and thirty five joined the church.

In the spring of 1817, the Spirit descended again and a considerable number were brought into the light and liberty of the gospel. It continued its gentle influences for more than fourteen months. In which time the society increased, backsliders were brought to remember their first love, to confess their sins, and move on in fellowship with his people, and many converts have been added to our communion. In June 1818, we purchased the Albany Theatre, and fitted it up for a place of publick worship, and opened it on the first day of January 1819. Thus, this church and congregation, by the benevolent assistance of their fellow citizens, and publick benefactors, have been instrumental in one short season, of sweeping away and burying for ever, one of the proudest ensigns of unhallowed ambition, that was ever exhibited upon the banks of the Hudson. This event has been ominous of millenial achievements, of national regeneration, and of the redemption of the world.

Upon the very day this house was opened, the Spirit descended, and his regenerating influences were felt and one soul at least, heard the voice of Christ speaking within his troubled mind, saying, Son, *be of good cheer thy sins are forgiven thee.*

It is now a most solemn time in this city. Let a stranger enter any congregation within this metropolis and look over the crowds that seat themselves to hear the word; and he will see a more than usual attention, and anxiety among them to know the things of the kingdom of heaven. And in some congregations he will hear sighs and behold hundreds in tears, before a sermon is closed.

There are but a few congregations out of the eleven established in this city, but what (according to my best knowledge obtained from the pastors of the churches and my daily observation,) feel more or less this heavenly dew.

I find every minister labouring under the same embarrassment with myself, when interrogated concerning the work in his congregation. We cannot tell how many are labouring and heavy laden under a sense of their sins. About two weeks since, I knew of only four or five in my congregation who were under very deep distress of mind, and now a large number are willing to own that they have been under awakenings for some time. Almost every day some new cases appear, and some soul is made willing to be saved, entirely, by grace abounding through the blood of Jesus.

For many months I have discovered a solemn and gradual work among the Presbyterian congregations, and an earnestness in their preachers for the reviving presence and power of Christ, that led me to believe, that the reign of heaven was approaching.

Since the commencement of 1815 one hundred and thirty one have been added to the first Presbyterian church, upon examination, and to the others, considerable additions have been made. To the Baptist more than one hundred, and many by letters to all the churches. Many candidates are examined, and are now coming before the churches in this city. At our next communions, we expect to receive accessions that will gladden the hearts of the righteous, and swell the songs of angels in heaven. Surely we can say, *The Lord is merciful and gracious; slow to anger, and plenteous in mercy. He will not always chide; neither will he keep his anger for ever. As far as the east is from the west; so far hath he removed our transgressions from us. Bless the Lord, all ye his hosts; ye ministers of his who do his pleasure. Bless the Lord, O my soul.*

—————

In times of revival, converts have a vast variety of sensations and are inclined to make these known in some suitable way, for the advancement of truth, and the happiness of their fellow beings. The following was written by a young lady in

Newark (N. J.) 2d March 1817, on the reception of a letter from her friend in Philadelphia.

Nothing could have come more timely, or been more acceptable : it arrived at a moment when darkness, thick darkness enveloped my mind : even the trembling hope that I had cherished, was gone : and I was a wretch most miserable, without a God, without a Saviour ! I had been examining myself as closely as I was capable, by the sacred word; and finding so little light, so much corruptibility, a heart still of unbelief, that I had passed sentence upon myself:—concluded that it was my understanding alone that had been convinced, while my heart was opposed to God and every thing good. I read in the Bible, that when the soul was indeed regenerated, *Old things would pass away, and all things become new.* These, however, I attributed to reading, reflection, and instruction. I was looking to my dear S——, for that great flood of light which I expected must enter the soul that is born

of God. O! that sentence of yours: Praise
the Lord for the least ray of light, even,
if you can see *men as trees walking*. How
it covered me with shame and confusion!
It was then I felt I had robbed the Almighty; and with heart-felt sorrow and
humble gratitude, I hastened to ascribe
glory unto God, for what he had done for
so vile and undeserving a creature. At
that moment my heart delighted in ex-
claiming, *Bless the Lord, O my soul, and
all that is within me, bless and praise his
holy name.*

But where I have one moment of joy, I
have hours of sorrow; though, even those
precious moments have afforded me more
real happiness, than all the pleasure of my
past life summed together! Pleasure did
I say of a past life? There is nothing that
I can look back upon that deserves the
name. Vain world, thou art indeed a de-
ceiver! O! I have loved thee, dearly loved
thee: but what hast thou to give in return
for all my servitude and affection? Ah!
what pierces me to the heart; a life thus

far lost—worse than lost. But my Dear S——, this world has lost its charms: I can see nothing in it that now attracts me, or inclines me to live for it.—My wishes, desires, and hopes are soaring far above it. Give me but my Saviour, and I have no wish left ungratified; One kind assuring look, and I ask no more. But O! the thought again, that my *heart is deceitful above all things.* My experience may be a delusion—yes, and a delusion which may follow me through life, and even to the grave, and which nothing but the voice of the Judge of heaven and earth shall awake me from! Distracting thought! to cry, *Lord, Lord, I have prophesied in thy name, I have eaten and drunk in thy presence:*—but he shall say unto me *I know you not whence you are.* O! pray that the great Searcher of hearts would search me, and that he would carry on the good work which I humbly hope he has begun in my soul until death. If he leaves me I am lost; nothing short of Almighty power can save. Into his hands I rejoice to commit myself. O! I would be no where else for worlds. Let others do as they may, I am resolved to serve the Lord,—if I must perish, I perish no where but at the foot of the cross, crying for mercy. When I shall see you, I will tell all the Lord has done for me; though that would be almost impossible. But you know the value of the soul, have seen and felt the evil of sin, and have found yourself delivered from it; you can fancy what my feelings are. I have been left to my own evil heart and the temptations of Satan for some weeks past, and horrour indescribable took possession of me. My trials as well as my joys I will tell you. But thanks, everlasting thanks, to our glorious Conqueror, who enables me to say, and I believe sincerely,

Jesus my God I know his name.
His name is all my trust.

And you know his name too, for you have tasted and seen that the Lord is good; you have heard those blessed accents fall from his gracious lips, *Daughter thy sins are forgiven.* O! eternity will be only boundless enough, to sing the praises of such a Saviour. When, in my imagination, I behold the inhabitants of heaven casting their crowns at the feet of Immanuel, and crying, *Worthy is the Lamb that was slain, to receive power, and riches, and wisdom, and strength, and honour, and glory, and blessing;* my heart overflows; and with rapture, with extacy indescribable, I exclaim with the poet,

> There I would vie with all the host
> In duty and in bliss,
> While less than nothing, I could boast,
> And vanity confess.

But who am I that am allowed to indulge such hopes! It appears almost impossible. I dare not think it—I who am viler than the vilest: less than the least—one who has so long, and so obstinately refused—one who has sinned against such light and knowledge—one who has indeed been exalted to heaven in point of privi-

leges, and who verily deserves the lowest
hell for abusing them—me to whom a gracious Redeemer has stretched out his arm
all the day long, crying, *turn ye, turn ye,
why will ye die?* Yet my obstinate, obdurate heart has refused all my life long these
tender, these blessed exhortations.

I have turned a deaf ear; or if an answer was given, it was *I pray thee have
me excused!* Surely I am a living monument of the long-suffering and tender patience of our God. O! his forbearance
with me—how wonderful! May my spared life be devoted to Him who died to
save my wretched soul. I have not told
you any thing about the revival in this
place, and my letter is almost finished. O!
that you were here with us, enjoying this
precious season—why not come and gladden our hearts? I am sure you would be
compensated for any difficulties that you
might encounter. The precious Saviour
is still with us, carrying on his work gloriously. It is supposed that about five
hundred are under exercise of mind; and

many have obtained *a good hope through grace.* It is a day of power and mercy. O! that we were wise, that we would consider this. Remember me in you prayers.

QUESTIONS.

Have you seen yourself to be, by nature and practice, a lost and helpless sinner? ——Have you not only seen the sinfulness of particular acts of transgression, but also that your heart is the seat and fountain of sin; that in you naturally, there is no good thing?——Has a view of this led you to despair of help from yourself; to see that you must be altogether indebted to Christ for salvation, and to the gracious aid of the Holy Spirit for strength and ability rightly to perform any duty?

On what has your hope of acceptance with God been founded?——On your own reformation?——On your sorrow for your sins?——On your prayers?——On your tears?——On your good works and reli-

gious observances?——Or has it been on
Christ alone, as your all in all?——Has
Christ ever appeared very precious to you?
——Do you mourn that he does not appear more so?——Have you sometimes felt
great freedom to commit your soul to him?
——In doing this (if you have done it) has
it been, not only to be delivered from the
punishment due to your sins, but also from
the power, pollution, dominion, and existence of sin in your soul?

As far as you know yourself, do you
hate, and desire to be delivered from all
sin, without any exception of a favourite
lust?——Do you pray much to be delivered from sin?——Do you watch against it,
and against temptation to it?——Do you
strive against it, and in some good degree
get the victory over it?——Have you so
repented of it as to have your soul really
set against it?

Have you counted the cost of following
Christ, or of being truly relgious?——That
it will cut you off from vain amusements,
from the indulgence of your lusts, and

from a sinful conformity to the world ?——
That it may expose you to ridicule and
contempt, possibly to more serious perse-
cution ?——In the view of all these things,
are you willing to take up the cross, and
to follow Christ, whithersoever he shall
lead you ?——Is it your solemn purpose,
in reliance on grace and aid to cleave to
him, and his cause and people, to the end
of life ?

Do you love holiness ?——Do you love
a Holy God, and because he is holy ?——
Do you earnestly desire to be more and
more conformed to God, and to his holy
law ?——To bear more and more the likeness of your Redeemer ?——Do you seek,
and sometimes find communion with your
God and Saviour ?

Are you resolved in God's strength, to
endeavour conscienciously to perform your
whole duty—to God, to your neighbour
and to yourself ?——Do you perform common and relative duties conscienciously,
as part of the duty which you owe to God ?

Do you make conscience of secret prayer

daily ?——Do you not sometimes feel a
backwardness to this duty ?———Do you at
other times feel a great delight in it ?——
Have you a set time, and place, and order
of exercises, for performing this duty ?

Do you daily read a portion of scripture,
in a devout manner ?——Do you love to
read the Bible ?——Do you ever perceive
a sweetness in the truths of holy scripture ?
——Do you find them adapted to your ne-
cessities, and see, at times, a wonderful
beauty, excellence, and glory in God's
word ?——Do you make it the man of your
counsel, and endeavour to have both your
heart and life conformed to its doctrines
and requisitions ?

Does the glory of God ever appear to
you as the first, greatest, and best of all
objects ?——Do you desire to promote the
glory of God, as the chief object of life ?

Do you feel a love to mankind—such as
you did not feel before you became religious ?——Have you a great desire that
the souls of men should be saved, by being
brought to a genuine faith and trust in the

Redeemer ?——Do you love God's people with a peculiar attachment—because they bear the Saviour's image, and because they love and pursue the objects, and delight in the exercises, which are most pleasing and delightful to yourself?——Do you from your heart, forgive all your personal enemies, and refuse to cherish or entertain any sentiments of hatred or revenge?——If you have injured any person, have you made reparation; or are you ready and willing to make it?

Do you feel it to be very important to adorn religion, by a holy, exmeplary, amiable and blameless walk and conversation?——Do you fear to bring a reproach on the cause of Christ?——Does this appear to you extremely dreadful?——Are you afraid of backsliding, and of being left to return to a state of carelessness and indifference in religion?

Do you desire and endeavour to grow in grace, and in the knowledge of Christ your Saviour, more and more?——Are you willing to sit at his feet, as a little child, and to submit your reason and understanding, implicitly, to his teaching; imploring his Spirit to guide you into all necessary truth, to save you from all fatal errours, to enable you to receive the truth in the love of it, and to transform you, more and more into a likeness to himself?

COUNSEL.

Remember that these questions are intended to point your attention to subjects of inquiry the most important. Do not, therefore, content yourself with a careless or cursory reading of them. Read and deliberate, and examine yourself, closely, on each question, and let your heart be lifted up to God, while you are considering each particular, in earnest desires that he may show you the very truth. You cannot ordinarily go over all these questions at one time. Divide them therefore, and take one part at one time, and another at another. But try to go over the whole in the course of a week; and do this every

week, for some months. When you find
yourself doubtful or deficient, in any point,
let it not discourage you: but note down
that point in writing, and bend the attention of your mind to it, and labour and
pray till you shall have made the attain-
ment which will enable you to answer
clearly. It is believed that you cannot
fail to see how each question ought to be
answered.

Remember that secret prayer, reading
the word of God, watchfulness, and self
examination, are the great means of pre-
serving comfort in religion, and of growing in grace. In proportion as you are
exact and faithful in these, such usually,
will be your inward peace, and the safety
of your state. Unite them all together,
and never cease to practise them while
you live.—Think often of the character of
Enoch, and try to walk with God. Read
Mason's little book on self-knowledge,
Owen's works, Baxter's Saints' Rest, Dod-
dridge's works, Edward's works, Hopkin's
works, Gill's works, Bellamy's works,

Newton's works, Witherspoon's works, and Scott's works, &c. &c. *

Do not suppose that any evidence which at present, you may think you possess, of a gracious state, will release you from the necessity of maintaining a constant vigilance in time to come: nor from repeated examinations and trials of yourself even to the end of life. Many marks and evidences of a gracious state are set down by pious writers. But they must all come to this—to ascertain what is your prevalent temper and character—Whether on the whole, you are increasing in sanctification, or not?——If you are, you may be comforted; if not, you have cause to be alarmed. It is only he that *endureth unto the end that shall be saved.*

I think it of very great importance to warn you not to imagine that true religion

* Some of the works in President Green's catalogue, I have omitted and added others, which I hope will be found of equal merit by all who can obtain, and carefully examine them.

is confined to the closet, or to the church; even though you apprehend that you have great comfort and freedom there. Freedom and comfort there, are, indeed, most desirable; but true religion reaches to every thing. It alters and sweetens the temper. It improves the manners. It goes into every duty, relation, station, and situation of life. If you have true religion, you will have a better spirit, you will be better sons, better scholars, better friends, better members of society, and more exemplary in the discharge of every duty; as the sure consequence of this invaluable possession. And if your religion does not produce these effects, although you may talk of inward comforts, and even of raptures, you have great reason to fear that the whole is a delusion, and that the root of the matter is not in you.—*Herein*, said the Saviour, *is my Father glorified that ye bear much fruit, so shall ye be my disciples.*

Be careful to avoid a gloomy, and to cherish a cheerful temper. Be habitually cheerful; but avoid levity. Be very humble. Be not talkative. Before experienced Christians be a hearer rather than a talker. Try, in every way, however, to promote religion among your relatives and friends. Win them to it, by your amiable temper and exemplary deportment.—*Flee youthful lusts.* Shun every excitement of them. Guard against dissipation : it extinguishes piety. Be not disconcerted by ridicule and reproach. Your Saviour bore much of these for you. Think of this, and be ashamed of nothing, so much as of being ashamed of him. Trust in his protection, live to his praise, and you will dwell eternally in his blissful presence.

FINIS.